W 9/8 S2

West
American

S0-BRO-975

O. J. Grimes,
Salt Lake, Utah.

1917 — 1st ed. VG. teg. 197 p. fold map.

683

56443378 00

3C-7

Threading the Royal Gorge

Courtesy, the Denver and Rio Grande System

Going Abroad Overland

Studies of Places and People in The Far West

By

David M. Steele

Rector of the Church of St. Luke and The Epiphany,
Philadelphia

"Go far; too far you cannot. For, the farther,
The more experience finds you. And go sparing.
One meal a week will serve you and one suit
Through all your travels. For you'll find it certain
That, the poorer and more lowly you appear,
The more things you will see through."

BEAUMONT & FLETCHER.
The Woman's Prize, Act IV, Sc. 5.

Illustrated

G. P. Putnam's Sons
New York and London
The Knickerbocker Press
1917

The Knickerbocker Press, New York

Foreword

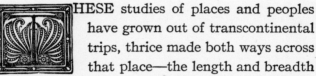HESE studies of places and peoples have grown out of transcontinental trips, thrice made both ways across that place—the length and breadth of the United States—inhabited now by one people. They were written on three summer outings in that number of years past. Their purpose has been to acquaint the denizens of Eastern districts with their neighbors, far removed but close allied, their fellow-citizens of the Far West.

The while these chapters were in course of composition, I have traveled twenty thousand miles. To ride on railway trains six thousand miles and more on each of three six-weeks' vacation journeys may seem a queer method of resting; but that must be set down to inherent queerness and allowed to pass at that. So also must other peculiarities in choice of theme and mode of treatment. In truth, it has been play to do this work—though work it was; for the chapters were written first as weekly articles for the Religious Page of the *Philadelphia Press.* This may seem the only point they have in contact with religion; but that again is the author's affair and the publisher's privilege.

If either the book were less pious or this preface more polite, I would dedicate the volume to my congregation. As it is, I am going to give it to them instead. It is prepared as a Christmas present to parishioners. It is for sale only to others. In all grave formality—although without daring to ask their permission—I dedicate it to a wholly different group of friends: to one special coterie who go to church less and need it more than any rogues I know; to the staff of that newspaper office where they first were published.

I inscribe it, therefore, to that rare fraternity. I dedicate it to editors, compositors, typesetters, proof-readers, staff-men, space-men, press-men, correspondents and cartoonists, cub-reporters and copy-boys. They may not want to read it; they have had to do that already. They will not need to buy it; they have earned it in the course of their

day's work. They may not even like the "dedica-
tion." But I like it. And the reason is that I
like them.

D. M. S.

PHILADELPHIA, PA.,
   Christmas, 1916.

Contents

Illustrations

ix

Going Abroad Overland

Going Abroad Overland

CHAPTER I

Going Abroad Overland

BETWEEN two certain long journeys, the one across the ocean and the other across the continent, there are such points of similarity as warrant this phrase for a title in this descriptive narrative. For one thing, the distance is about the same. It is three thousand miles, roughly speaking, from the Atlantic seaboard to the coast of England; it is just about that far from New York to San Francisco. And the time consumed in travel is about the same. The fastest steamers make the one trip in five days and a fraction; it takes the fast express trains just about that long to make the other.

The choice of routes presented also is identical. There is a northern and a southern and a middle one. The first passes far up through the wheat and forest belts and comes out on the bleak Norway-like coast of Oregon, or farther, at Vancouver or Prince Rupert; the second, as far south, to reach the sunny, soft Italian clime of Southern California; the third, the middle course, across the prairies, plains, and mountains, to the coast at San Francisco.

In certain minor points also the two trips are alike, points none the less striking. For example, one may have his choice of first-class, second-class, or steerage comforts (or discomforts) in the Pullman, tourist, or day coaches. As he keeps on west, for five days, in one straight course, as he would east on the other, he must change his watch from Eastern time to Central, then to Mountain, then Pacific—five hours' change—else he will find himself as far off one way as he would the other way in London.

There are sights and sounds, too, that remind him of the sea. A worn-out freight car on a side track is a derelict; tramps riding on the bumpers are true stowaways; the mystery of signals, semaphores, and colored lights is equal to that of St. Elmo's fire; while here and there a yard with a dis-

abled engine, wrecked freight cars, loads of scrap
iron, and great heaps of rubbish, look like wreckage
on a storm-tossed shore.   And when one gets far
out, there are those limitless expanses of prairie,
with no boundary save the great curve of the
ocean-flat horizon, and those ranges of great mountains where the grades go up and down at times so
steeply that the train in taking them seems to
pitch and, rounding curves, to roll until, if one be
imaginative enough, he can get car-sick and think
that he is sea-sick—which will make the parallel
complete.

.It was ten o'clock that July morning when I
climbed aboard that westbound Fast Express and
dropped my suit-case by seat Number 7.   The car
was half full and it would be fuller; for the train
was the road's favorite.   All about the car there
was an air of most mysterious politeness; for the
passengers, while all restrained and deferential
toward each other, were solicitous and curious;
we were strangers now but we would be together
for five days and must perforce become acquainted.

Inside the car, the porter was ubiquitous, the
newsboy omnipresent, and the passengers engaged
with both.   Outside, friends who must stay behind

called in good-byes through open windows, baggage men rushed trucks of tardy trunks toward the forward car, while up ahead the engineer was stroking his impatient iron steed.   Apart from all, cool and collected, stood the stern blue-clad conductor with one hand holding his watch, the other raised to give the signal for departing.   At length the long stentorian "all aboard" was sounded and with warning bell and hiss of steam escaping, the engine strained toward its task.   Slowly at first it threads its way through the maze of tracks in the yard, as though undecided which one of a score of pairs to choose; but, when it has made up its mind, its pace increases gradually until that well recognized sound of the galloping wheels on the crossties and rails proclaims that it has struck its normal gait and—we are off.

One who goes traveling nowadays is surprised at many things, but chiefest of all at the number of people who keep him company.   This may be due to many things.   It is due mainly, however, to one thing—that is, our modern changed conception of this as a means of education.   It used to be said of a person: "He is well educated; he speaks so and so many languages."   Now it is said of a man:

"What an intelligent man he is. Why, he has traveled. . . ." And this estimate is accurate; for there are things one cannot learn in any other way.

Of these one is geography. There is a certain sense of location, a familiarity with things as they are; a feeling of identity and reality which can never come in any other way save from the seeing of them. And, just as charity begins at home, so should the application of this principle. It is perfect folly for any civilized American ever to cross the ocean in search of landscape beauty or of nature's wonders until he has first seen what his own land has to offer. Americans by the thousand annually cross the Atlantic, to climb the Alps, to scale the Matterhorn, to view the beauties of the Rhine and Rhone, to bask in the sunshine of Italy, and to indulge in the delights of rural England, France, and Germany, seemingly unaware that their own country contains attractions of mountain and forest, river and lake, sunshine and pure scenic beauty as far surpassing those across the sea as our own mighty continent surpasses tiny Europe.

And to see that country, to gain any conception of its size, of the abundance of its resources, the grandeur of its scenery and the virility and versatility of its people, there is no other way so effectual as to ride those five or six days in one journey across its whole length and look out upon it and its people from a car window.

The special route we took lay first across the Keystone State then the great State of Ohio, along the shores of the Great Lakes, through cities also great, across the vari-colored garden farms of Illinois, the Corn Belt of the Middle States, and the great prairie ranches farther on, across the Mississippi, true "Father of Waters"; over the Rocky Mountains, real "Alps of America"; across the Alkali Desert, and up, and then over, the Sierra Nevadas.   The course was sometimes in a line for miles as straight as the flight of an arrow, then again round mountain curves so sharp the engine seen through the car window at our elbow seemed to have rebelled and started back; yet always in the end it pressed on westward.   Here for miles our course would lie along the bases of great cliffs and cañons and through narrow mountain passes where one could scarcely see daylight above, and there along the brinks of precipices which measure their depths not in mere feet and inches, but in fractions or in multiples of miles. Pressing onward thus, we followed the course of the setting sun, which after each day's contest won the race and set far on ahead to leave us in the dark. Night after night the train continued on into this darkness as though still impelled by the momentum of its hard day's run until again it was challenged by the rising sun another morning, to begin the race all over and to continue it another day.

Not among the least important of the things one learns and the new impressions he receives on such a journey is a new and great respect for the railroad itself; both for a railroad as an institution and for railroading as an occupation. On a long journey such as this one, after seeing any great railroad in all its length and any such system in all its wondrous workings, one decides that more wonderful even, if possible, than the country these roads traverse is the human genius which in sixty years has shortened the journey across it from half a dozen months to half a dozen days instead, and the still greater genius which, coupled with faithfulness and fidelity, have made that rate of speed commensurate with safety.

But most surprising of all and worthy of consideration by itself, is the luxury of modern railway travel. The very practice of vestibuling cars has given a sense of luxury in that it gives a sense of security; it closes snugly in one's comforts and closes out discomforts of ill wind and weather. Indeed it is this very art of keeping clean which, under a disguise, is the art of not becoming fatigued. And not only is this luxury a modern fact; it is, in large measure, a national trait. As one rides through the far West and Southwest, the contrast between the appointments of the palace car inside of which he rides and the poverty and dirt of the Mexican "Greaser" outside, furnishes a striking illustration of the difference between the Anglo-Saxon-American and the Spanish-Latin-American types of civilization. These fast through trains are really swift-moving hotels. Think of electric lights, hot and cold running water, easy chairs, a writing desk, a library, a bathroom, a barber shop, a dining-room, and spacious sleeping compartments, all whirling through the landscape at the rate of fifty miles an hour!

More interesting even than the railroad itself, more so than the country through which it has passed—or than the people aboard of its trains

even—are the increasingly novel sights that may
be seen each day from the car windows as the train
runs farther and still farther west.   Some of these
are small things; some are great and bold and striking.   All are interesting because never seen before.
It is the seeing of them that gives one a sense of
their reality, increases his vocabulary, and gives an
actual content to words he has heard used all his
life.   Hereafter, in his mind, these words will
connote real things.   We saw a trail, a ranch, a
range, a corral, a cyclone-cellar, a "bunch" of
cattle and a "band" of sheep; we saw a "shack,"
an irrigation "ditch," real prairies, and real mountains.   And we looked at each one with a new surprise and viewed them each one wonderingly.

We saw for the first time some great sights also;
lurid burning straw piles at night as we passed
through the harvest fields; titanic chasms, sky-
high peaks, giant redwoods, and a thousand things
all on a scale the very sight of the size of which
should make the men who live habitually in sight
of them big men—as indeed it does.   Here and
there we saw that remnant and reminder of an
earlier day, a lonely "prairie schooner," toiling
westward.   We saw old men stop work in fields

and look at it.   They may have thought back on
the hundred days they once spent, fifty years ago,
in coming west by that method themselves.
They could retrace that path now in half as many
hours.   But they have never done it.   And they
never will.   They came to stay—and they have
stayed.

Thus on and on for five full days we traveled.
On the morning of the sixth, by one of those sudden
reversals and contrasts for which the country here
is famous, we dropped down of a sudden from the
winter region heights of the snow-clad mountains
into the very heart of summer verdure, where the
grass is always green and flowers bloom all the
year.   As we crossed the bay on the ferry-boat
and came up to the dock at San Francisco I looked
at the clock overhead and noticed what to my
mind was the last and withal most surprising feature of the journey—that which would not happen
in any other country in the world, nor with any
human venture undertaken by other than Americans: we had traveled three thousand miles with
safety and comfort and were arriving at our desti-
nation on the very second of the very minute of
the hour the schedule read.

CHAPTER II

Following the Setting Sun

 AM writing this from California. I am one of many travelers; for more tourists are crossing the continent this summer than any other ever heretofore. Some of these are seeing America first, and quite as many of them last, the Exposition at San Francisco drawing the former, the European war, which has precluded foreign travel, driving the latter. All will return the better for their going, better because broader in their vision, bigger because of the enormity of sights they look upon, wiser in their understanding of the land they have traversed, and with a sympathy they have not had before for fellow-members of their kind.

I have come myself, almost without stop, from the Broad Street Station to the Railway Portal in Los Angeles, from the City of Brotherly Love to the City of the Angels. And it has been literally an ascent from earth to heaven. Almost continuously one's moods succeed each other in a heightening crescendo as he passes from each strange scene to a yet more novel prospect and finds hope fulfilled that each new day will lead him through a district richer and more varied in sights never seen before. Daily, upon an average, one turns one's watch back and that often, roughly speaking, the scene shifts as there succeed each other regions agricultural and arid, historic or romantic, scenic or pictorial. At least this is certainly true on the far southwestern route I traveled.

This Santa Fé line taps the most fertile farming sections of the United States. It has opened up regions rich beyond belief in mineral wealth. It goes through the heart also of romantic America, the Land of the Conquistadores and Padres, of the Pathfinders, Traders, and Pioneers. There is some of the most remarkable scenery in the world on this passage and there are enchantingly interesting special sights to see along the way. There are literally a hundred places to stop over for a day deserving a description of a thousand words apiece. Stops might be made with advantage wherever the sun goes down offering a Thousand and One better than Arabian Nights' Entertainment.

But this is a study rather in broad generalities. I can reconstruct as from a dream the league upon league long changing kaleidoscopic pictures passing hour by hour outside the broad car windows. We swept through, from Chicago, the wide agricultural districts of Illinois, Missouri, and Kansas, the Rocky Mountain lands of Colorado, the picturesque Indian haunts of New Mexico, the geological marvels of Arizona, and the old Missions of California, on to San Diego for that matter, where the sun shines every day, where flowers bloom every season, and where grass is green the whole year round.

We left acres by the million of waving corn and wheat and found these giving place to other areas apparently earthwide suited to cattle and horse and sheep raising, these to alfalfa and sugar beet culture, as many to grazing as farming of both kinds, and as many in all to the plants of the desert. As we watched them, fences appeared to vanish, forests wholly to evaporate, and land to come on in which there is not on an average so much as one stone to a county. Sunflowers gave way to sage-brush and later this to cactus and mesquite, while barnyard fowls were chased by prairie hens and farmers' pet canines by prairie dogs and these last in turn by jack rabbits, reversing all the laws of evolution as we looked off backward from the flying platform of the observation car.

Out across the long flat prairies, drab barns with no roofs succeeded red barns with brown roofs as these in turn had replaced the prosperity proclaiming new white painted buildings of the Middle West with their ubiquitous red roofs above the green which both so suitably surmounted. Then, when we were certain we should never see again a human habitation, there began adobe houses in the desert, culminating in huge patios with pergolas. Across state boundaries, windmills and straw piles gave place to water tanks and snowbreaks, while long lines of telegraph poles ran away off to the far horizon as though demons of the air were after them. In the places where once were but poverty, danger, and death, there are now the vast projects of land reclamation, conservation of forests, and asylums new found for—best of all—quick, sure restoration of health. There are square miles by

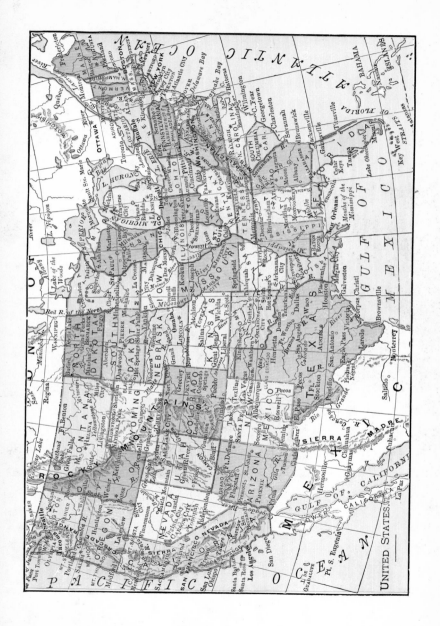

UNITED STATES.

the hundred, yes by the thousand, still awaiting the rain that will never fall, still in need of the proverbial water and good society; but, even in these, irrigation has made gardens out of portions as broad as some eastern States.

We began to see Swastika emblems at the bounds of Colorado, signal that we would soon enter the land of the Navajo and Chimayo, the Zuni, Hopi, and Laguni, with their arts and crafts and handi-work of blankets, baskets, beads, and bracelets, wickerwork and earthenware; while the Indians had scarce become familiar figures before they were crowded off the stage of station platforms by dark Mexicans and these in turn by Japs and China-men. Lo, the poor Indian! Sometimes he is low, but sometimes nowadays quite the reverse. We saw them in all stages, from the grimy, vermin-ridden tobacco beggars, squatting by the depot, to the dapper Carlisle-graduate hotel clerk, even owner of the same, and to his brothers who have sold their oil rights and ride into town in their own autos—to the movies.

But the chiefest features of enchantment through a long strength of this veritable El Dorado are the physical features and natural phenomena thereof. This breeziness begins with the plains portion of Colorado, with its rarer air and clearer sunlight, where we first caught sight of Pike's Peak fifty miles away. Across this high, broad uplift, with its rising mounds and rocky hillocks, on far through New Mexico and Arizona, it is no exaggeration when the advertisement folder proclaims "A mile or more in the sky for most of the way." Alternating come far glimpses of snow-capped serrated ranges through the clear, pellucid air and near-at-hand marvels that call for cameras to supersede field glasses. There are the romantic Spanish Peaks and here the tragic near-at-hand Enchanted Mesas. Off a few miles is the Petrified Forest, and farther stretch hundreds of miles of the weird Painted Desert, of which the colors are nowise exaggerated in the figments laid on pictures of them from the artist's palette. Thousands of acres are covered with agatized fossil remains of gigantic prehistoric trees about Adamena, while Flagstaff is point of departure for many places by automobile and pack horses, where Cliff-dwellers have left, in pueblo and in kiva, writings graven on stone walls and implements of household usage and Aztec ruins and hieroglyphs that astonish archæologists. From here on a great volcanic uplift begins that brings you over a gigantic table-land to the Grand Canyon—earth's greatest scenic marvel.

Things are not all of this kind, however, and no chance obtains for monotony. The altitude of Arizona alone varies from 100 feet to 13,000 feet above sea level, so that within its own borders there is every zone save the most humid tropics. There are steep and high red-colored cliffs and mesa fronts, then fields as fertile as a new-found Eden. There are fruits of all kinds that are cultivated and, *per contra*, every member of the cactus family, from the diminutive "Fish hook" to the giant Sagurdas that reach a height of fifty feet. On through Southern California we came joyously, surprisedly, to Pasadena, the "Crown of the Valley," at the foot of the Sierra Madre Mountains, where—think of it!—the Rose Tournament is held on New Year's Day. At San Bernardino also is a strange study in contrasts: the largest railroad shops west of Topeka stand in the midst of the orange groves of the San Gabriel Valley.

Which prompts one to perplexity: whether of twain is more marvelous on this whole journey, the

2

works of nature or the works of man? To build
this railroad for two and a quarter thousand miles;
to run palatial trains across the desert, this is an
accomplishment. But more, to have built a
highway where no man had traveled, and that to
connect lands wherein no man dwelt, that was a
work of faith, the substance of things hoped for,
the evidence of things not seen. But they are now
apparent and on a scale more unbelievable. The
development of this half of a hemisphere, and in
scarce more than half a century, is the eighth—
aye, the eighteenth, wonder of the world.

I recollect some figures in mixed order but in
statement of plain fact, that attest the unexampled
progress of our people and the marvels wrought by
masters in fields both mechanical and mercantile.
Of this Santa Fé System alone, with its main-track
mileage of 11,306, and traversing thirteen States,
a book might be written, showing how the little
railroad which started west from Topeka in 1869
has become a great transcontinental system, with
annual gross operating revenues of $111,000,000.

One has forgotten the inferno of Pittsburgh's
environs and his disgust with the ramshackle sight
of Chicago's approaches by the time he has reached

the corn belt and the interminable wheat fields of the States anent the Desert. He swoops across the fertile and expansive width of Illinois, athwart the rich black billows of loamy Missouri, and he finds himself again in fields where wheat shocks stand so thick they look like an eruption on the flesh of fecund soil. He is within the Sunflower State, which is no longer Bleeding Kansas, but an empire in itself, deriving last year $186,000,000 from one staple only of its multiple crop acreage. He is less confused by the commingling as he goes on, of windmills, grain elevators, cyclone cellars, gang plows, and corn cultivators, trees in rows for windbreaks and checker-board rectangled roads all full of automobiles, than he is when silver dollars take the place of paper and the salesmen cease to make change for a nickel. He views the novelty of red flat foreground in the picture and the mountain-spread perspective, sees empty alkali basins and sponge-cake stratas where the railway cuts begin in Colorado, rides through arid regions where the train seems to risk death for all aboard by thirst and to court slow starvation, where the soil is the color only of the gophers that infest it with their little burrows, and then suddenly slides into an oasis, where is a Fred Harvey Eating House and where a dapper little Japanese bellboy is making a noise like a bee swarm on a dinner gong.

He remembers some things he has seen in passing; but he knows that greater works than these are yet to come. He has crossed the Mississippi on a bridge two thousand feet long. He has ridden through the Union Passenger Station in Kansas City, with room for 10,000 passengers at one time. He has learned that Iowa's crop of corn alone was 340,000,000 bushels last year, with a value of $200,-000,000. He has passed a single freight yard up in Colorado where last year a million tons of coke were shipped. He sees hundred-thousand-acre ranches, million dollar this and hundred million dollar that, and decides that he is, in very truth, living in a Billion Dollar Country. Then he thinks of what that country is to be. He comes into New Mexico, of which the coal deposits alone are greater than those of Belgium and France combined. Last of all, his traveling companion mentions irrigation—this as they come in sight of the Rio Grande.

This one river alone, from the Colorado line to the Mexican border, has a fall of 3500 feet. The

waters already are impounded under a United
States reclamation project. The reservoir formed
by the Elephant Butte Dam is now the largest
artificial body of water in the world, the capacity
being 2,642,000 acre-feet, or 862,200,000,000 gal-
lons—enough water, if spread out, to cover the
State of Delaware two feet deep.

And what is the contrast between old and new!
Before the railroads came, all commerce from
Missouri River points westward was carried on by
caravans of pack mules and wagon teams. The
most notable highway across the prairies was
known as the Old Santa Fé Trail. This railroad
we have ridden on now follows that same route
and supersedes that method. There were so
many conflicts with hostile Indians in times afore-
said that detachments of United States troops
went along to guard lives and property. Now
where are they both? The earlier caravans of
pack mules numbered seventy-five to two hundred
animals and made fifteen miles a day. An average wagon load was five to seven thousand pounds
and an average day's journey seventeen miles.

In 1846, 375 wagons were employed, also 1700
mules, 2000 oxen, and 500 men; this was increased,

by 1866 to 3000 traders' wagons. During the
height of the traffic 50,000 ox-yokes were used
annually. The largest train was composed of
eight hundred army wagons carrying supplies for
General Custer's Indian campaign in 1868. The
first overland mail coach started from Independence, Missouri, for Sante Fé in 1849; in the early
sixties daily stages were run from both ends of
this route. Each Concord coach carried eleven
passengers, the fare being $250. The trip re-
quired two weeks. To-day, on a railway train,
the journey consumes only fourteen hours, and
the railroad fare is about $25 one way, as many
hours now as it then took days and at about one-
tenth the cost. Behold how hath God wrought
and what man has accomplished!

CHAPTER III

The City of the Holy Faith

MONG the many matchless scenes of Nature's making and the things of monumental size, the outdoor scenery and sights of modern man's achievement, in the Great West—cañons, rivers, plains, and parks, big trees, vast reclamation projects, caravansaries and expositions—it is good to find, if only by comparison and for relief by contrast, a historic center that is as important in its way, as unexampled in America as all these others are, for that matter, in all the world. I mean the Old City of Santa Fé.

The seasoned traveler of two continents, after he has compared the attractions of both, is wont to make admissions of grandeur in the new-world places of his pilgrimage; but he will usually regret that places in this country lack the atmosphere that age alone can give. Well, that depends. It depends upon whether he has or has not seen this

region. In this series of articles I am reverting so
often to places and things of the former class that
it is a joy to find the land I travel through this week
containing at least one of the desired and desirable
second class, one that ranks equally with others
of the first in its own special manner of importance.
Indeed, it is a place not only of historic, but of
prehistoric interest.

In this portion of the great Southwest is this
one corner with the coloring of the Orient under
Andalusian skies, in a setting older than that of
Babylon and Damascus. Something of that in-
tangible air of mystery that the Moors brought
from the East to Granada was transplanted from
Mexico to American soil by the Conquistadores.
Here, among scenic surroundings that must have
reminded them of their Iberian home, blossomed
the City of the Holy Faith, the capital of the Sunshine State, and the most picturesque city of the
United States. And yet this ancient civilization
was built on another, equally as picturesque but
thousands of years older. Far back beyond this
old old Pueblo culture is a substratum that imagination has pushed back to the very birth of mankind, the Cliff- and Cave-dwellers whose twenty

thousand cave and cliff dwellings puzzle the archæologist with their well-preserved ruins and remains.

Santa Fé is the capital of New Mexico. But that is unimportant, compared with the many other things it is. It has fine large sanitariums and regal homes for wealthy invalids, in which, as well as being center and distributing point for lesser of the same, it reminds one of Saranac Lake. But that again is not its primary claim to importance. Those who would see three realms at once, without danger and without far travel, Spanish Mexico, our own entire American Indian life, and the best that remains of the whole Frontier West, who would learn the history of conquest for three centuries, read the entire romance of their country's early settlement, from the Louisiana Purchase through the gold fever of '49, and the military occupation of the Southwest in Apache and Buffalo Bill days, and who in addition would rest while they study and regain health while resting, let them go to Santa Fé.

Here focus an unusual number of lines of interest, each one of which in kind has made some other place world famous. Among them, for example, are at least these things: its historic background, its romantic story, its monuments and reminders of three wars, its relics of frontier encounters, its reminders of overland trail days, its environs full of prehistoric people's works and worship, its ideal climate, its paradise, not far removed, for fishermen and sportsmen, its position now as stopping place between the Painted Desert, the Petrified Forest, the scenes and settings of snake dances and other strange orgies of the Indians, the Grand Canyon and, last of all, the sunny land of Southern California.

This region, little known as it is, has not gone wholly unobserved nor unappreciated. It will be more heard of and as well known soon, as it richly deserves. It will be preserved for one reason alone: on this Jemez Plateau, skirting the Rio Grande del Norte, there are found habitations of prehistoric man in great ruin centers suggestive of cities.

Around these cluster the pueblos of Indians who represent a civilization antedating the discovery of America. The result is an area of greater archæological and ethnological value than any other within the United States. To preserve this area as a field for scientific research and as a recreation ground for the people of the United States, bills have even now been introduced in the Senate and in the House of Representatives proposing to create of this area the National Park of Cliff-Dweller Cities.

The principal charm of the story of life here written at present is Spanish, but all that is only since it was prehistoric. The tone of its present-day life is Mexican rather than American and the population is Indian rather than either. The architecture is "mission" and the building material is "adobe." But the great point is the wide diversity of its attractions. Here is a city that has scenic, ethnologic, historic, and prehistoric interest. Here are stored old Spanish archives covering two and a quarter centuries and numerous paintings of great age. Here was outfitted a regiment to serve in the Mexican War. Here stand the ruins of Fort Marcy, on a hill outside the town. Here volunteers from Colorado, together with natives and cowboys, saved the Southwest to the Union in a bloody two days' battle.

But, most important of all, here ended, in the old frontier days, before the railroad's coming, the

famous, blood-stained, toil-sanctified, and skeleton-
strewn Santa Fé Trail. At one corner of the
Plaza, the old adobe house still stands which was
once fortress, tavern, trading post, and rendezvous
for all types to foregather when, with cavalcade to
guard them across the dreary plains, the old stages
from their trip across the desert with its dangers
drew up, inclosed in dust and laden with adventurers.

And yet, early as was that date and long forgotten as are its peculiarities, this city is older by
far than this century even. It was an established
city before the Pilgrims landed at Plymouth. It
was known adown the western portion of the continent before Jamestown had become a permanent
abode. For, in 1606, Juan de Onate, one of the
Spanish Conquistadores, founded his capital here
on the ruins of two small Indian pueblos. It was
the northermost point to which the Spaniards
pressed in 1540, as it later became the western
terminus of the old transcontinental trail.

Nineteen American and seventy-six Mexican
and Spanish rulers have successively occupied its
palace. Here it was, incidentally, that General
Lew Wallace, while Governor of the Territory,

wrote *Ben-Hur.* The city has survived all those
strange modulations by which a Spanish province
has become a State of the Union. The story of
the palace stretches back into real antiquity; to a
time when the Inquisition had power, when zealous
friars of the Order of St. Francis exhorted throngs
of dimly comprehending heathen, and when the
mailed warriors of Coronado told marvelous
uncontradicted tales of ogres that were believed to
dwell in the surrounding wilderness.

San Miguel Church is believed to be the oldest
church building in the United States still used for
public worship. Built about 1607, destroyed in
1680, rebuilt in 1710, it has been renovated now in
recent years. In the rear of the auditorium stands
a bell cast in Spain in the fourteenth century. The
altar painting is more than six hundred years old.
Adjoining it is the oldest cemetery in the Southwest. Tradition has it that the remains of De
Vargas lie under the altar.

Here, therefore, as a result of these many districts' convergence, is the most wonderful fifty-mile
square in America. This palace of the Governors
is the oldest government building in the United
States. The names of the two hotels, the De

Vargas and the Montezuma, give hint of the people's pride in their antiquity. And the people themselves are unique. On these streets I was not once asked for alms, pestered for backsheesh, nor was I served by any one obsequiously for a tip. They are a proud and self-respecting lot, these people, with their American thrift and frugality and with their old-time Spanish pride in leisure. They have new-world industry with old-world sense of aristocracy.

There are wonderful environs also all about, with this as center, for a dozen or two dozen miles. There are good trout streams in many cataracts of the upper Pecos. That stream itself glides through sylvan dells, to reach which one passes through many and picturesque Indian villages. A vaporous view of the sunset, as the train ascends the Glorieta Divide, reveals the reason for the impressive, not sacrilegious name, "Blood of Christ Mountains." With an altitude itself of seven thousand feet above the sea, the city is yet the center of a plain around which mountains rise on every side, towering to heights 10,000 to 13,000 feet. At an altitude of 9600 feet, a scenic highway has been built by convict labor up the Canyon,

The Old City of Santa Fé

over the Dalton Divide and down Mancho Canyon. All about are the ruins of historic pueblos, as at Pecos, discovered by Coronado in 1540, at San Cristobal, and at San Marcos. There are pueblos inhabited to this day, linking the old and the older in one civilization, as at Tesuque, Santa Clara, and San Ildefonso.

Points of prehistoric interest are Pajarito Park, the region west of the Rio Grande, with twenty-thousand cliff dwellings scattered through its numerous cañons. The most interesting of these is the Frijoles Canyon, with the ruins of prehistoric communal houses of which the most important are Tyuonyi, a circular shaped structure; Tsankawi, with deep trail worn into rock by human feet; Otowi, with the largest pottery accumulation found on the plateau; Puye, containing over one thousand rooms on the ground floor of one structure; the Ceremonial Cave; the Painted Cave; the Stone Lions, an important prehistoric shrine, and the Stone Tents, peculiarly shaped rocks in a branch of the Otowi Canyon.

Points of scenic and general interest are Santa Fé Canyon, with Monument Rock; Big Tesuque Canyon, with Tesuque Falls, Nambe Canyon, with

Nambe Falls; Pecos Valley, famous for scenery, hunting, and fishing; Lake Peak, 12,380 feet high; Baldy Peak, 12,623 feet high; Canyon Diablo, a short but rugged cañon; Crater, 180 feet deep, amidst a lava field; La Bajada Hill, presenting one of the finest views of the Southwest; the Petrified Trees; Glorieta and Canoncito, famous battle fields; and Turquoise Mines, the oldest in the United States, now owned and operated by Tiffany's, New York.

Ultimately this whole region is to be restored. The traveler will be able then to wander through once buried cities older than Pompeii. Just at present, a quite practical and feasible thing is being done and to the advantage of all concerned. A consistent plan is being adopted of having new building, much of which is being done, carried on along the lines of old-time architecture, so that the new city yet to be will duplicate in its appearance and design the older one that was, and this part of New Mexico, at least, be a true replica of the old. Santa Fé is coming into its own rapidly, this urban center of the antique time, and for the most modern of reasons. It is this. The National Old Trails Highway should naturally follow, as chief course

of all, the Old Santa Fé Trail, should it not? And
so it does. To-day this town is a wayside stopping place on the automobile route from Baltimore
to Los Angeles. Think of that, ye who count
distance in the East.

Are you an invalid? Here are outdoor sanitariums and hospitals. Are you a lover of Indians?
Within a few hours' ride are several Pueblo Indian
villages, dating back before the Spanish Conquest.
Do you like Mexican life? The soft-syllabled
Castilian tongue is spoken on every street corner.
Is mountain scenery what you want? Ride out
along the scenic drive, toward Las Vegas, to the
headwaters of the Pecos. Are you by nature
devout, and does your interest in things devotional
increase with reverence for age and your enthusiasm
rise for those old padres, missionaries, spiritual and
patriotic adventurers at once, who first planted the
cross on the continent? Then these few para-
graphs may give you motive and material for
much reflection.

3

CHAPTER IV

Grand Canyon, Titan of Chasms

HERE are more Philadelphians in this hotel to-day, the El Tovar, at the Grand Canyon, than at any hotel of its size in Philadelphia. Last night there were eighty odd registered. All these have come three thousand miles. And that is less than half the distance of the round trip they are making. Which minor two facts seem to illustrate two major ones; namely, that this is an unprecedented year for Western travel, and that this place is well worth a visit. Eighty times three thousand miles is the distance from the earth to the moon. That is considerable mileage. Yet that represents only one city's quota, for one day, at one point in a hundred, where this summer tourists are foregathering by myriads.

I forgot to say the day is Sunday. That fact is of importance. These eight hundred persons all told here, from all points, are a larger congregation than in any of eight hundred churches at this moment in the places whence they came. And well may this be so. For this Titan of Chasms is, in its power to compel one's moods, in its sublimity and majesty, in its awe-inspiring size and in its utter weird unearthliness, eight thousand times more marvelous than any domed cathedral ever yet constructed. In the power it has to sober men in presence of infinitude, in the effect it has on flippancy and in the way it melts small human pride to modesty and calms the turmoil of life's stress by its size, by its silence, and most of all by its age, it is efficient beyond any man-made sanctuary. It is such a place as has no parallel elsewhere on earth. It is a service in color, a sermon in stone, a prayer in its depth, a petition in its far flung reaches of the unexplored; while, in the echoes from its all but fathomless abyss, there sounds the deep-toned chant of Judgment Day.

I will not attempt description. Every one who comes here disavows ability—and then goes home to do the very thing they had foresworn. They try but to fail utterly. The reason is there are no adjectives of size commensurate. All passing on of observation second hand depends upon similitude; and to this there is nothing similar. No wonder that the aborigines on this part of the continent who, like the Sadducees knew neither angel nor spirit, yet believed that this place was Heaven—and Hell. It might be either, for it looks like both. Here their God made his dwelling place and here ours has disclosed his handiwork. He did this once, in this one place, and ever since and elsewhere He has rested from such work of revelation. And shall man depict it?

How describe a chasm that is two hundred and seventeen miles long, thirteen miles wide, a thousand feet more than a mile deep, painted with all colors of the rainbow, clothed with light as with a garment, beautiful by day as the Hesperides, and at night so yawning, so sepulchral, so dark and abyssmal as to look like nothing short of Tartarus.

But, there! I said that I would not try, and am determined to be the exception that shall prove the rule. Just one paragraph, in borrowed language—and that by a Japanese. Says G. H. Corse, of Yokohama:

Niagara Falls is wonderful; Yellowstone Park is delightful in mountain scenery; Mammoth Cave in Kentucky is "spooky"; the Himalayas are grand as the roof of the world, and the Taj Mahal at Agra in moonlight is the most beautiful sight in India. I have seen them all. But to gaze at Grand Cañon is to be "gripped" in heart and soul, the like of which I never before experienced in all my life. I am going back to this place on my next visit home.

The first and possibly the most astonishing thing the traveler to Grand Canyon experiences is the fortunate nature of the approach to it. There is absolutely nothing to apprise you that the place is nearer than a million miles, until you step out of the train right at its edge, almost right into it. A hole more than a mile deep at the side door of a railway station and hotel which you have entered from an absolutely level course across the desert from the railway junction sixty miles away, is enough to cause heart palpitation. And it does. You have changed cars at Williams, Arizona, where the air is the color of ether, where it blows as cool as though electric fanned and is so ozone laden that it cures tuberculosis, but where every other prospect is unpleasing, and where Mexicans are vile. You ride for two hours through scenery that has for features two water tanks twenty-five miles apart, of which the inhabitants are one jack rabbit on an average to each telegraph pole, and the un-commercial products of which are, apart from the mesquite and cacti, a few stunted piñon and gnarled desert growths.

At length, of a sudden, these give way to a thickening, heightening clump of scrub pine and dwarf cedar which grow thicker still and higher as though to screen jealously from your unholy eyes the sight they are compelled reluctantly to disclose. The train takes the upgrade slowly with a growling, grinding protest and comes to a sudden stop. You are at the gate of Heaven: you look to the depths of Hell.

I had been to Grand Canyon before, but only as a tourist for a day. That was the thing to do ten years ago. Then, people stopped between two trains, stopped, looked and listened, marveled at the scene or complained of the cost, according to their depth of soul and past experience of travel. Some looked on speechless until they fainted or prayed; the rest ran away to buy post-card pictures of it and inscribe them with cant phrases of approval. To-day all this is changed, both the place and the people: the latter are the best, the most appreciative, this because most cultured and

The Grand Canyon

intelligent, of really leisure-loving, nature-worship-
ing, long-distance travelers, and the environs have
been so transfigured and accommodations multiplied that these can stay on now in comfort and
explore the place as it deserves. A week or two
weeks' stay now is more normal. Even this is
scant time enough to "do" the whole region.

I stopped long enough to marvel, before I
explored old scenes anew, at changes that the hand
of man has wrought here where the works of nature
gave him courage and begat in him conviction
that this would become a "resort" rather than
merely a stopping place. It is a tribute to the
despised tourist class who are accused of haste
and levity, of sacrilege and shallowness, this fact
that things are planned here of such spacious size
and with such permanence of substance. And the
builders have their faith rewarded. I came out
upon a quarter-million-dollar hotel, its appointments those of any city hostelry.

I counted lesser tabernacles for those less affluent,
enough to house them, or to tent them rather. In
garages stood, and through the forest roads there
ran, sea-going automobiles by the score. A power
plant serves the premises that would supply a

Middle Western city.   There are mules and horses
for the trails and liveries that would fill a ranchman's corral, while, beyond the station, there are
miles of sidings where long trains of solid Pullmans,
four, five, or six sections to one schedule, each one
with two engines, are equipped to haul two thousand persons in or out per day.   This resort has
"arrived."   And there arrive here daily and stay
weekly, monthly, notables from all four quarters
of the habitable earth.

To come these many miles, half way around the
long mid-continental summer circuit of migration,
stay only one day and flee off, were like the famed
exploit of the King of France or of one, Merkle,
in his halting haste at Second.   This were not to
touch the Canyon.   Be it said therefore that nowadays the average visitor stays longer and does more.
He loiters about the hotel a few days until he
gets his bearings and gains reassurance that, if
he does not fall in, the monster will not open its
vast jaws the wider just to swallow him.

He first takes the Rim Drive along the most
unique scenic roadway in the world, westward to
the head of Hermit Basin, seven or eight miles.
He views the Desert Palisades north of Grand

View and times his arrival of an evening at Hopi Point, noted for its sunset. Here he can stand away out on a thin solid wall, thrust like a spear into the lengthy monster's inner side, and look down and across until he is as dazed as he meant to be boastful. Next he will essay Bright Angel Trail, descending that marvel of corkscrew construction and having his recompense in thrills of every conceivable kind. He then outfits and goes camping for a day, a night, or both, in a "rough camp," or as smooth as he wishes—and will pay for. As his courage rises and enthusiasm heightens, he explores afoot or horseback, on his own account and everywhere. All ways, at all times, he will have the Canyon itself for companion and object of study. But, instead of diminishing, it only grows larger the more he looks upon it and, instead of divulging secrets, grows the more secretive the more he pries into its past history.

From the stone-constructed Lookout, where a huge telescope boxes in the panorama and brings it in sections under microscopic measurement, one may spend hour upon hour. Even without aid of lenses other than his eyes or magnifying agency else than the sparkling air, one can see

but not until then, the Colorado River began to cut the Grand Canyon through the lower third. If that was the end of the work of Creation, when must the beginning have been?

CHAPTER V

A Sunday at Lake Tahoe

HAD never heard of Lake Tahoe until Fate picked me up and literally led me to it. I was amazed, as are all other tourists, to find a region of such varied charm so easily accessible from a transcontinental trunk line, yet so little known by travelers from the Far East. It is fifteen miles from one of the mountain stations on the main line of the Southern Pacific Railway, central route, two hundred miles inland from San Francisco. Here is not one thing alone, but a whole coterie of things delectable: water, mountains, rivers, lakes, forests—and climate.

This huge chest of Nature's art treasures is as awesome as Niagara, as interesting as the Yellowstone, as different from other places as Yosemite, and its beauties are those of the Thousand Islands or of the Muskoka Lakes. The country about the lake is of the wildest kind as far, so it seems, as the

distance the sun travels over, and the name itself,
appropriately chosen, is old .Indian for Great.
People plan here to stop off a day and they stay for
a week or a month.   Nor are the reasons far to
seek.   They may be summarized in four words,
viz.: climate, topography, healthfulness, and restfulness.

High mountains above and wide water below,
the snow-covered hills for a frame and the lake for
a picture; these two features dominate.   Then
come all the details.   The height of the mountains
is irregular; but they stand a perfect circle of fine
scenery.   The depth of the water varies from a few
feet to over 2000 feet; which, together with the
peculiarly variable bottom of the lake, produces
marvelous color effects.   The lake bottom on a
clear, wind-quiet day can be clearly seen, except in
the lowest depths.   Here and there are patches of
fairly level area, covered either with rocky boulders,
moss-covered rocks, or vari-colored sands.   Then,
suddenly, the eye falls upon a ledge, on the yonder
side of which the water suddenly becomes deep
blue.   That ledge may denote a submarine precipice, a hundred, five hundred, a thousand feet
deep.

These colors and this beauty are nothing else than words from Nature's gospel. Is it not wonderful, the way in which something unspeakable and unexplainable covers the chasms and wounds of the earth with splendor? Is it not what the name of the lovely New Hampshire lake, Winnepesaukee, indicates: "The Smile of the Great Spirit"? It is noteworthy that this color is connected with purity. The green ring of this lake is so brilliant, the blue enclosed by it is so deep and so tender, because there is no foulness in the water. The edge of the waves along all the beach is clean. The granite sand, too, often dotted with smooth-washed jasper and garnet and opaline quartz, is especially bright and spotless.

But, to turn description into narrative. It was on this wise. There were five of us: "Pop" and "Doc" and "The Domine"—and the two others. All had set out from Philadelphia; it was by merest accident that we foregathered at the St. Francis in San Francisco. The first named was a well-known mining engineer, in whom there is no guile; the surgeon was the mildest-mannered man who ever cut a throat or scuttled an appendix; Madame W. is a grand dame who knows as many interesting

people as she tells good stories of them all; and
Viola, her daughter, has a nature that becomes
her name.   In this mode consorted, we were on
our way returning from the Panama-Pacific Exposition.

Thus made we our pilgrimage. We came, by
early morn, to Truckee, above Sacramento, which
is junction for the puffing little narrow-gauge line
up the banks of the clear, tumbling river, between
mountains high as Nebo, to the Lake with its far
vistas.   Between ways of travel long ago and now
is scarce a greater contrast than that, by reversal,
between the great Mallet locomotive that had
brought us on the main line and the little busy-
body wood-burning contraption that, slipping
and apologizing, drew us up the cañon.   For it
took both time and patience to ascend that long
defile.

The lake itself is rightly called the Lake of the
Sky, since it is the largest lake of its size at its
altitude—twenty-three miles long by thirteen
broad, 6225 feet above the level of the sea—with
but one exception in the world.   It covers about
190 square miles, and its watershed is about five
hundred square miles.   The boundary line be-

tween Nevada and California strikes it on the
northern border, at the 120th meridian, a point at
that spot being called the State Line Point.

It is easy to fall into superlatives; but the sight
disclosed at the end of that morning hour was
nothing short of superfine. Above the Lake there
was the clearest sky; around it breathed the purest
air; framing it stood the sharpest peaks, perpetually snow-crowned; while the water itself had
the hue of indigo, except where the shale beaches
gave to it cromo tints of every color of the rainbow. Best of all, the whole place had an atmosphere
of calm repose and restfulness. Perhaps it is the
confidence it has in its own high superiority that
it imparts to travelers and makes them feel at
peace.

In the whole region, the days and nights of
summer are free from both wind and frost. The
sun so tempers the air that every hour is an ex-
hilaration. Is this because or in spite of the fact
that near at hand you are embowered in forest and
that in sight all about you are those snow-clad
ranges? These forests of trees have a charm in
themselves; pines, firs, spruces, hemlocks, cedars,
junipers, and tamaracks. The native populace

4

were Washoe Indians and these are the only
habitants that brave the winters.   Others clear
the way early for King Cold.   And an early setting
in it is, they say, of his long reign.

But this summer climate certainly is as near
perfection as is conceivable.   The days of sunshine, clear and bright, are crowned with soft,
beautiful sunsets, while the nights are cool and
sleep-inducing.   This is a place where woodland
and mountain breezes cool and purify the air to
such a degree that it has a subtle charm.   Here is
a place where the scenery is beautiful and romantic
where nature is at her best, nature glorified, nature
almost deified.

All about the region there is such hunting in
season as consists in finding and such fishing as
exceeds stories that even proverbial anglers tell.
For, above all else, there are trout.   About a ton
a day are taken from the lake, in the season, for
purposes commercial.   We tried to fish an hour by
the way, upon an outing one day, in a little stream
along the auto road; but the trout seemed wiser
than we.   Last year the prize trout taken from the
lake, for which a silver cup is offered every summer,
weighed twenty-eight pounds.

There are two main things to be done by those
who "do" Lake Tahoe. Other excursions by the
dozen may be taken; these two must be taken.
They are the boat trip and the motor trip. The
steamer excursion goes on a circuitous journey
once a day, touching at all the little ports and piers;
and any one of half a dozen automobile routes there
are by which cars run, preferably to Emerald Bay
and thence on to Tallac and return. We did these
both, and by each were impressed, either giving a
different vantage point for viewing the weird
beauty of this sheet of water and those mountain
heights.

On that complete circuit of the lake by boat new
glories and fresh wonders constantly sprang forth
as pleasant surprises and we learned to realize that
here Nature indeed has been most prodigal in her
scenic gifts to mankind. The shore all along is
indented with deep, curved bays and coves, bor-
dered by narrow sandbeaches, and where the sands
end the steep mountain sides rise right up aloft into
space—rise up like vast walls a little out of the perpendicular and thickly wooded to the point where
the timber line gives way to snow. The water is
so shot through with light that you can see the

bottom anywhere down to a depth beyond your former power to believe, while the beaches, shelving sometimes and sometimes precipitous, produce all shades of green by their various depths of color.

Chief of all the automobile trips is that boulevard ride around the lake to Tallac, and thence on by Lakeside and by Cave Rock to Glenbrook, a distance of fifty miles; which same we took, and on which we often experienced, on looking down from one of its many mountain galleries, a feeling of surprise, as if the sky and earth had somehow been reversed, as if we were looking down upon the sky instead of on the earth.

There is something else here as unique as anything yet mentioned. Maybe I am long in coming to it, since it seems the thing most in my line; but so was Sunday long in coming. No one here, however, is late, nor even neglectful, in attendance at a service in a most peculiar church. The Church of the Transfiguration is unique, in that it is an open-air building, the altar only being roofed. Towering pines stand as aisles and the vaulted ceiling is the clear blue dome of heaven. Rustic and simple, it harmonizes exquisitely with its surroundings and strangely insensible must that worshiper

The Apache Trail of Arizona
Courtesy, Southern Pacific Railway Co.

be who, as he kneels in this Nature shrine, with a wonderful accompaniment of hundreds of singing birds and the ascending incense of a thousand flowers, does not feel his own soul lifted into a higher and more spiritual frame.

CHAPTER VI

The City without a Soul

AM spending this third Sunday, on this summer journey, in Reno, Nevada. Of all places on earth's surface in which to find theme for fitting discourse upon matters religious, this might, perchance, seem the most unlikely. And it is—unless there be some value in extremes and force of emphasis in the selection of a subject for religious study by sheer contrast.

It was an old saying in pioneer days that there was no Sunday west of the Missouri River and no God west of the Mississippi. With fond loyalty to its early tradition, this State of Nevada bids fair to prove the abiding truth of both above assertions. As for God, one may be here or hereabouts; but, as for Sunday, that is literally an unknown institution.

I have spent Sundays in many regions out in this far Western country through summer vacations.

I have found themes, some in works of nature, some
in types of human nature, all because they merited
discussion from the point of view of one who sought
for good in everything and felt he wrote for read-
ers who could find religion even outside churches.
But here is a novel setting. If certain of those
topics had to do with Heaven, or with things
celestial, this one hints by way of warning at
another region, because things by contrast are so
diabolical.

This city is famous—or infamous rather—on
four counts: it is place, *par excellence*, of prize-
fighting, horse-racing, open gambling, and easy
divorces. Here is a spic-span city, up-to-date,
progressive, modern, concrete-paved, electric-
lighted, full of stores and shops with goods of
quality. Not a vehicle in the whole city is not
gasoline driven or electrically propelled. It is
populous and prosperous, yet the center of a
population of pickpockets and procurers. It raises
its revenue from race-track and from prize-ring,
open gambling halls and Sunday baseball. It
is truly a place, not of liberty, but of license. It is
city-center of a land of limousines and lawyers' fees
—of luxury and alimony.

Yet withal, it is a pleasing city. It is a synonym for everything progressive, up-to-date, and *fin de siècle*. It lies—rather it stands—at an altitude of 4500 feet. It is 250 miles from San Francisco. It is the county seat of Washoe County. It was named in honor of General Reno who was killed at the battle of South Mountain. It is attractively situated on the Truckee River at the eastern end of the base of the Sierra Nevada Mountains. It has a fine courthouse, a still finer jail, good business blocks, better hotels, a number of houses that are fairly palatial, and all its homes are handsome residences. It has excellent public schools, a model library, a few—yes, even a few—churches, and the State University buildings are on rising ground outside the city's limits.

Reno is the distributing point for a large freight business to a prosperous country community; this is because it is surrounded by an extensive area of agricultural, albeit irrigated, land. All round about are irrigation projects, where the devices and industries of men have made the desert blossom as the rose. And this it is, among other things, that has made its citizens so rich. It is the center for an important stock-raising industry—

and this gives it its love of horses. It is entrepôt for the interior of a State of vast mineral wealth—whose denizens dig gold and silver without stint of measure and look only for high-priced ways and for pleasing places where to spend it. There are brick and tile and stone and concrete buildings, streets, and pavements. There are fine, smooth, straight boulevards. In short, it has all the aspects of a modern city.

Yet I recall most clearly—as perforce must every visitor—two places in particular: the Casino at the Riverside Hotel and the Grand-stand of the State Fair and Racing Association. This means I have been trying to make here a study of a two-fold theme, divorce and gambling. My impression is that they are closely allied. The truth is, matrimony of the kind that is only temporary, and merchandising of the sort that is made by bookmakers, seem to have many points in common. At least they are indulged in certainly by the same people. How far either is the effect or the cause of the other, it remains for some philosopher to settle as a problem in eugenics and finance— or maybe financial eugenics.

I went to the races. I do not mean I went

to-day—but yesterday. What for? Well, I did not go seeking amusement. I have had that years ago. I did not go to wager; that were an expensive luxury. Nor did I go to study social problems; that is the poorest pretense and the lamest excuse of all those who sniff at vice, but, daring not to bite, do hope for heaven. Well, then, why did I go? And, pray, why should I not? I ask myself as much as you. Would you have done it? Would you not?

Which points a curious perversity of human nature. It is not our reasons—it is not even our excuses—that explain our actions. It is what we bring out of them that gives detriment or value, hurt or profit, to experiences. I went solely from curiosity—as you would. I came back feeling four things, which feelings will stay with me always. I was impressed with the extent and amount of poor human credulity; the amount of this is pitiful. I saw novel types of femininity; the number of these is disheartening. I observed debauchery of youth, especially of children—and this is distressing. I was moved to mirth, and then to wrath, at the commingling of groups that ought to be segregate—and this last is disgusting.

Reno. Courthouse and Riverside Hotel

I have made up my mind that the whole State of
Nevada, so far as the regulation by its laws is
concerned, might as well be one wide race-course.
This town might be called, without doing violence
to the truth, a municipality of assignation. This
city as a whole compares with Monte Carlo, and
the "only four games allowed" would be sufficient
for a Canfield's place at Saratoga. I said at the
outset that this moral teaching is by contrast.
Those four vices illustrated are all of such horrid
mien as to be hated need but to be seen.

I have said that I did not go to the races to wager.
But few can afford that. If it is true that the
only way to make money is to save it, the only
way to save money here is to let all wagering
severely alone. There were crowds of people
betting who had not enough to eat at home. But
that is not the worst. These races are not run for
those alone who look on. They are nation-wide
as institutions, and reports of them are followed
by a myriad. Because of the four-hour difference
in time between the results made known here at
four P.M. and places three or four thousand miles
distant, you waited last night in Philadelphia or
New York hotels at your dinner between courses

while the waiters took side journeys between dining-room and serving pantry to steal glances at news-tickers. Such are the long tentacles that hold the gullible.

But these races make a strong appeal here to the populace, and on two counts: first, the admiration that the native of Nevada always has had for fine horseflesh; and, secondly, the fact that gambling has been native with him ever since the days of Bret Harte and Mark Twain. Racing without betting, to a ranchman or a miner, would be about as exciting as would mint be to the proverbial Kentucky colonel without julep. True, it is done nowadays by a new, a mechanical method. Machines of the pari-mutual type make the odds. There is small chance of cheating and little need for chicanery; but, even so, the bookmakers have not changed. How clever these creatures are! How alert, quick-witted, glib of tongue, and deft of fingers! They could make a better living doing better things. I have never seen such human waste of good material.

And yet the bookmaker is only one of many types of human being in this human maelstrom. There were possibly five thousand persons present

yesterday, a company as nearly without souls,
I think, as human beings can be. Every type
was represented, and all shades, degrees, and grades
of contrast. In the paddock there was range
extensive, from the coatless, beltless, shirt-sleeved,
and suspendered rustic to the silver-buckled, dia-
mond-scarf-pinned, flannel-trousered, panama-hat-
ted dancing-master off for an hour's outing from
the Dunn Pavilion. There were cowboys, ne-
groes, Japs and Chinamen, ranch owners, mining
magnates, stock-brokers, promoters, rich man,
poor man, beggar man, thief. There were judges
to watch the jockeys and detectives to detect the
bookies. There were types of women also—but
that is another matter. Oh, the sordidness, the
silliness, cupidity, and gullibility, the diabolical
ingenuity and the satanic sensuality of that whole
scene!

I set out, however, to speak of divorce. Well,
have I not? It is true that I have not philoso-
phized upon it; but, are these facts unrelated? It
is lamentable that the types depicted by those who
describe this city as a center of this industry
speak always in the femine gender. You will hear
only of "divorcées." It is they, alas, who are in

the majority. Which one fact gives emphasis to a
hard truth; namely, that the majority of divorces in
this country are sought not by men but by women.
And the still harder fact—hard not so much to
explain as to extenuate—is that the overwhelming
majority of divorces sought for the purpose of
remarriage, are by wives and not by husbands.
This it is that accounts for the gender of those who
come here to establish residence.

I picked up a panorama folder of views of the
city at the news-stand of the Union Depot. It is
not without significance that its cover design was a
photographic reproduction of "The New Court
House and the Riverside Hotel." Thus are
symbolized two leading industries. If rates at the
Riverside Hotel are low, they are synonymous
with those of that reputed hostelry in a town down
in Texas, "Board and Lodging Extra." And,
alas, judging from the types of women who are here
upon one errand, if decrees of divorce are costly,
as compared with the prices of marriage licenses,
my philosophic colored porter spoke truth when
he averred—speaking for himself of his experience
as husband—"But lah, boss, it's wort' de difference."

CHAPTER VII

The Mountain Cast into the Sea

HAVE spent this summer Sunday, of this the first week in August, worshiping—if such I can prove that it was—confessedly in a peculiar manner. That day brought me to Ogden, by morning, thence across the Lucin Cut-off over Great Salt Lake. I have spent days upon other journeys marveling at scenes in Nature which were graven by creative power of God; in this instance, I have marveled equally at something here constructed by the hand of man.

As I rode literally for hours across this structure where a "fill-in" has been made by engineers, of earth hauled from the hills to make this highway on the waters, there went singing through my memory a unique phrase of Scripture which in this quite novel fashion comes to have new and real meaning: "Jesus answered and said unto them, Verily I say unto you, if ye have faith, ye shall say unto this mountain, Be thou removed, and be thou cast into the sea; and it shall be done."

For such is the story in brief of what has been done here. And the whole accomplishment is a triumph of faith. A lesson proposed by this text— and taught here by this object lesson—is worth pondering to-day. This "cut-off" is a railway line laid in an old lake bed from Ogden, Utah, to Lucin, one hundred and three miles. Part of this lake-bed is dry; part is under water. The part under water is Great Salt Lake.

Our route all the way westward from Omaha followed the course of the tide of civilization that swept out to California in the golden days of "forty-nine." The pioneer always chose the shortest route, and to-day this railway follows in his steps. Merely to ride over this natural highway is to bring one into better understanding of the men who wrested the country from the Indian, the buffalo, the savage, and the sagebrush. But all this is said only in passing.

Our train had left Ogden and run westward fifteen miles, over a level and fertile country, before reaching this lake. A monster undertaking thereupon came under survey, the building of a direct line across the great body of water, with the purpose of avoiding the curves and grades of the original line running around the northern end. It was formally opened only a few years ago, after eighteen months' work. It saves 43.8 miles of distance, 3919 degrees of curvature, and 1515 feet of grade. The sharpest curve on the new line is one and one-half degrees as against ten degrees on the old. The heaviest grade is twenty-one feet to the mile, as against ninety feet on the old line. For this saving, this one railway spent $4,500,000.

The line runs seventy-two miles on land and thirty miles on rock fills and heavy trestle work. The east and west arms of the lake are separated by Promontory Point. The first is nine miles wide, then five miles across the point, including a cut of three thousand feet, followed by twenty miles over the west arm of the lake. The lake itself covers two thousand square miles, is eighty-three miles long, fifty-one miles wide and, in the deepest places, thirty feet deep. It is the most salty sea on earth except the Dead Sea. The curves the new line saves would turn a train around eleven times. The power saved in moving an average freight train, because of lower grades, would lift an

5

average man eight thousand five hundred miles.

Fifty years ago and more, some very brave and able men decided they would build this first railroad across the continent. They builded westward from Omaha and eastward from San Francisco, the story of that building being one of heroic achievement. But in 1868 they came to this flat, broad bed of sand and salt and the great lake in the center that barred the way. So they built the track around the lake to the north. But a third of a century later there came to be so much more business; engines grew five times as large as at the first and freight cars came to carry five times as much weight. Where one train formerly ran each way daily, now sometimes a dozen each way climbed over Promontory Mountain. Every day, because of grades and curves, trains were lifted that much higher and carried that much farther than would be necessary if the road were built in a straight line. So the railroad men looked at the old grade over the mountain and then at the level way across the lake and decided to build a straight, level line, over land, through water, in spite of all obstacles, or overcoming them rather. Even the sea could not withstand such faith.

Lucin Cutoff over Great Salt Lake

Courtesy, Southern Pacific Railway Co.

Of the twenty-seven and a half miles through water, nearly sixteen were to be a solid ridge of earth sixteen feet wide at the top and seventeen feet above the water. Instanter set to work great steam shovels where an arm of the mountain runs down into the lake, and at Hogup Mountain, sixteen miles west of the lake shore—which mountain came up through the level cover of the lake bed—also at Little Mountain, on the east shore of the lake. Each shovel picked up seven tons at a scoop. Soon whole trainloads of rock and dirt were moving to make a solid pathway through the water. The mountains were being removed and cast into the sea.

Three thousand men went to work at one time. At night they worked in the gravel pits by electric light. In the cold of winter and the heat of summer there was no stopping. Steadily the solid pathway grew. Then came the great pile-drivers and the wooden piles. All told, 38,256 trees were cut down to make piles for the great trestle. A forest of two square miles was transplanted. The floor of that trestle alone is sixteen feet wide, and the lumber above the piling would make a board walk four feet wide and an inch thick from Boston

to Buffalo.   The Cut-off for one hundred and three
miles is more nearly level than an ordinary floor.
For thirty miles the grade is so slight that an average person would need to travel a half mile to rise
his own height.

And, too, something else besides the Scripture
passage quoted above comes into my mind.   It is
the striking identity between certain points in
this modern accomplishment of one, a great con-
structive railway builder, and the feat of one,
an ancient, in a century long antedating even the
whole Christian era.   When, in 481 B.C., Xerxes,
the son of Darius, would improve upon his predeces-
sor's method of invading Greece, he did so by cut-
ting a canal across the head of the Ægean Isthmus
and bridging the Hellespont.   Consequently, it
was said of his army that "they sailed through the
land and marched over the sea."   He did the
one to avoid the dangers that beset his father in
rounding the promontory of Mt. Athos, as this
modern Xerxes, E. H. Harriman, did this other to
escape the grades of Promontory Mountain.   And
the two encountered some like difficulties.   Xerxes' Bridge of Boats, which with such care he had
constructed, as he was about to march from Sardis

was broken in twain by a storm. Herodotus
relates that "Xerxes was thrown into such a pas-
sion by this intelligence that he ordered the archi-
tects of the bridge to be put to death and the
Hellespont to be scourged with three hundred
lashes."

The scourgers carried out the order of their
master; and as they lashed the traitorous and
rebellious waters cursed them in "non-Hellenic
and blasphemous words," so Herodotus observes.
Likewise, when this gigantic task of filling with
steam shovels and flat cars the quicksand portion
of Salt Lake began, there was an accident that
threatened to be tragic. Just what language was
used none may know; for it is not matter of record.
But they could not find the bottom: the filling kept
on sinking. Yet, since faith prevailed, more rock
was ordered—and more mountain, and still more—
to be cast into the sea. And it obeyed. The result
of that obedience, pursuant to that kind of faith
which makes itself forceful by the aid of will
and of work, is the kind of success that now crowns
this achievement.

All which is allied to the subject of prayer
as the verse just succeeding the one above cited

draws logical conclusion from the premises of that text's illustration. "What things soever ye desire, when ye pray, believe that ye shall receive them: and ye shall receive them." That is to say, you shall have every answer to every prayer, provided prayer is uttered in firm faith; but, more than that, provided it is uttered in the kind of faith which makes you willing so to work that, for yourself, against all obstacles, obstructions, accidents, and disappointments, you go on believing that the thing can be. And so believing in yourself as well as in the worth of what you want, you will bring any miracle to pass—even though it be the removing of mountains and casting them into the sea.

CHAPTER VIII

In the Land of the Dakotas

T is the morning of the tenth of August. I am on my way across the continent and the train has just left Fargo, North Dakota. Any one who will review his school geography will rediscover that this town is on the west bank of the Red River and that this river is the eastern boundary separating this great State from Minnesota. Any one who knows also the agricultural divisions of this country knows that this center, between these two rich, fertile States, is almost the exact center of that region, extending for a thousand miles eastward and westward, across Wisconsin, Minnesota, and the two Dakotas, familiarly known as the Wheat Belt.

Last night before retiring I crossed the Pullman porter's dusky palm with shining coin and bade him wake me up this morning in time to ride out from here for two hours through this region on the rear car platform. When he shook me out it was just five o'clock and still so dark that I was more inclined at first to reprove than commend such literal interpretation of my bidding. But in less time than it takes to tell it, I had learned, what he had known from former observation, that the very sun itself, in this strange land of sudden transmutations, moves with such characteristic Western "hustle" that it comes up early and all of a sudden. For, before I had made even the hasty toilet necessary for a swiftly flying train platform across an as yet slumbering prairie it had grown bright, broad, clear daylight.

Emerging on the platform I can only stand and stare and breathe at first, reflecting that it is indeed a far cry from Thirteenth and Spruce Streets to this Minnehaha Valley in the Land of the Dakotas. As far as I can see, which by the law of visual angles on the curve of the earth's contour is, just as it is at sea, about eleven miles, the surface of the plain is level—absolutely level. It is even more literally so than is the surface of the sea; for there is not a single mound or hillock or depression as large as the slightest wave or billow would be on the ocean. The stillness, too, is striking; for the very sparkle of the sunlight falls, not as it might do at sea on the tiniest ripple even, but only on a perfectly placid surface. The sky above is so smooth also and the dome shape of its arch is so perfect that where it comes down all evenly at the far flat outline of the circle-like horizon, it forms overhead a perfect reversal of the scene below. It looks like an illuminated blue cover set down over some huge, round, yellow platter.

Nearer at hand and in detail the scene is one of beauty also. But nothing short of moving pictures and color photography could give any right conception of it; for movement and color are the chief two characteristics of the view presented by the ornamented landscape through which we are flying at the rate of forty miles an hour. I am at the moving center of a fixed and stable circle. And off in the distance? As far ahead and as far behind as the eye can follow there is the long straight line of the railroad's course; it vanishes either way in the shining perspective of the parallel rails. Above there is not a cloud in the sky; below there is not a blot on the landscape. Across there is not a spot to mar the vision, nor, at the circumference, a single break in the low sky line.

The whole plain looks like a reflection of the sky above save for a sharp contrast in color. The two things form a ceiling and a floor which meet in a circumference, the patterns being formed, by sections of wheat, some cut, some shocked, and more still standing. They look like the great stretches of some high ceiling, inverted, papered with designs which are reflections of the patterns of a carpet laid below. The very regularity of the whole is a striking figure. Everything is arranged in straight lines and regular patterns, especially the rows of wheat shocks where the grain has already been cut. There are no fences; for there are no fields, the whole State from this point appearing to be one single wheat field. There is no waste land; every square foot seems to be cultivated. There is not even a weed in sight; nothing but wheat, wheat, wheat.

Nor are there even people in sight, This may be because it is too early in the day; the fact is, however, this gives the harvested and ripening crop of yellow grain a weird, uncanny semblance as of something that has grown up to maturity all of its own accord, that has been cut at night by goblins or good fairies and left standing here as a jest in the clear, bright morning sunlight.

From here on to Valley City, forty miles away, the run is due to be made in an hour. We have entered the famous Dalrymple estate, the largest wheat farm in America, once comprising thirty thousand acres, under one management. This means one field unfenced extending over a region roughly speaking eight miles square. Here the work of harvesting is on in earnest and reaping machines stand as they were left last night when late falling darkness interrupted finally the harvesters' progress. Here and there, dotting the landscape so insignificant and isolated as not to appear until one draws near and then to disappear as suddenly in the distance when the train has passed, there come into view a few things that look like the marks of civilization.

They hint the fact that men, although out of sight, have been here recently. Yonder in the distance, for example, are windmills which mark the first attempts of these frontier inhabitants to chain the forces of nature and to make them do their work for them. Yonder at last comes into sight one lone human being. Nearer, in the foreground are reaping machines standing in a row where horses have been loosed from them, standing

along sections sometimes four miles to a side.   In
one of these lines I can count twenty "blinders"
standing one behind the other.

I am impressed in looking on this scene by two
thoughts that suggest themselves regarding the
future of this country: first, the wonderful population that it will sustain when this great State,
instead of being farmed in such enormous sections
as it is now shall be divided up into small estates
and cultivated in farms severally; and, secondly,
the possibilities inherent here of raising more and
more grain when a thirty-thousand-acre ranch shall
have become a thousand thirty-acre farms, a family
living upon each, and all this land in consequence
instead of being tilled as now monotonously year
after year and rendered barren by exhausting its
resources shall have rotation of crops and shall
be cultivated carefully.   When that time comes its
five million acres under cultivation will have
become ten; its twelve-bushel average per acre
will be forty, and its half-a-billion-bushel yield
annually will have been quadrupled.

It is impossible to write of this landscape de-
scriptively.   The theme is too large.   The subject
is too overwhelming.   The attempt submerges one

beneath a flood of adjectives. The swiftly moving panorama of the sights that come in view ought to stimulate of course one's powers of description. Maybe they would, if they did not come so fast as to intoxicate.

But they did come so fast on that special morning that the task of writing them became like the task of a war correspondent writing under fire. I find on looking at the pages of my note book that, from this point on, in trying to frame adjectives to characterize them and to phrase laudatory terms in which to speak of them, I so dulled my pencil point that it seems to have ceased making any mark at all. I must have so far yielded to enchantment that I failed to resharpen it. I remember, as the train struck its fastest gait, that in order to insure something like safety, I pocketed my pad, flung my pencil into the maelstrom of the whirling, swirling wind currents behind the railed-in platform of that observation car, clutched fast that railing, crushed my hat on tight and opened wide my eyes in wonder. I merely hung on and looked on. I had ridden thus for a full hour before I realized that I was standing in the same position looking on the same unfolding scene.

CHAPTER IX

Canadian Jasper National Park

 AM writing this letter from Jasper National Park, in British Columbia. I have made the journey over the new Grand Trunk Pacific Railway to and through this far off portion of Northwestern Canada. This new transcontinental line is open for the first time this year. To be accurate, a portion of a hundred miles, some distance west from here, connecting with the line back three hundred odd miles from Prince Rupert on the Pacific, is not yet open to passenger travel, save on a "mixed," and, to favored ones, on gravel and construction trains; which may give some idea of the region's newness and its novelty.

But nothing, save the sight of it, can give any idea of this portion of this mountain kingdom's grandeur. Here, upon the building of this rail route, the Dominion Government, coöperating with a patriotic loyalty, has set aside as a national

park a tract of five thousand square miles for the
preservation of the forests and the fish and
game peculiar to the region and to prevent forever
any desecration of the scenery which in its present
state is certainly sublime.

In reaching this point I have taken the newest
new-world tourist trek. I have ridden on the best,
because the newest—in its high standard scale of
initial construction—of the wonderful ocean to
ocean steel highways; I have traversed the last
that is ever to be frontier of the great agricultural
West; I have reached the last to be explored forest
wilderness accessible by rail, and now, at journey's
ending, I am in the heart of the least known and
yet best worth while knowing of the Northern
Continent's vast mountain regions.

Here is Mount Robson, which, according to the
Government authorities, is the highest mountain in
the Canadian Rockies; here is the Yellowhead
Pass; here are Brule Lake and Whirlpool River,
Maligne Canyon and Miette Hot Springs; here
are valleys green as emerald by hundreds, and glass-
clear, hard-as-granite glaciers, full as many, without name; here are half a dozen mountains that
stand out among a thousand having names all

unfamiliar, but with pinnacles above ten thousand feet; here is the Continental Divide and here, on one steep watershed, the fountain and spring sources of four mighty rivers—the Saskatchewan, the Athabasca, the Fraser, and the Columbia. Here is ultra-alpine scenery. . . . But what's the use?

It would be a futile effort, and a waste of time and talent—if one had them both—to attempt to frame new phrases in description when this has been done so well already, in such classic language, and by so many versatile writers. For, although the region is so new as to be yet unknown to tourists, it has been explored by certain pen-and-pencil trappers, by adventurous photographers, and by literary huntsmen in search of unseen scenery, for the past score or the past dozen years.

For example, Mr. A. O. Wheeler, director of the Alpine Club of Canada, in his expedition to the Rocky Mountain section along the Grand Trunk Pacific Railway, in Alberta and British Columbia, in company with a scientific party from the Smithsonian Institution, in writing of Mount Robson and the immediate neighborhood, gives a vivid impression of its unique and marvelous environs. Says he:

Mt. Robson from Grand Trunk Pacific

Courtesy, Grand Trunk Pacific Co.

Mount Robson dominates the district. It outtops and overrides all about it. But we are making a hundred-mile circuit about that great mass, and everywhere, on all sides, are mighty snow-clad peaks, widespread snow fields, huge crystal ice falls, rushing glacial torrents, leaping waterfalls, green, flower-decked valleys, and vast sloping stretches of spruce forest. You can have no idea of its immensity. I shall never lose my recollection of its grandeur.

Another speaks surprisingly who says:

There is really little ground for comparison between the Rockies here and the Selkirks. Everything here is on a larger and grander scale. These mountains are higher, more majestic and imposing. In fact everything is on a more magnificent scale. Nature has been lavish hereabouts in an extravagant distribution of grandeur. I shall never forget my journey through the Yellowhead Pass.

While still another goes into like rapture thus:

Here is destined to be the "Mecca" of the modern Alpine world. Banff, Paradise Valley, Lake Louise, Yoho and Glacier are spots long dear to the tourist's heart, but concentrated within the sweep of the base-line of Mount Robson are more beauty spots and wondrous scenery than in all the others combined. For aside from the mountain itself, with its high-flung, snow-crowned peak, its perpendicular walls of rock,

6

and its overhanging glaciers, the miles and miles of mountains which surround it are so full of interest that the region is destined to win world-wide repute.

In fact, there is every diversity here of natural features to delight and gratify the mountaineer or the explorer, to interest and to revivify the tourist. It is an expanse of indescribably sublime grandeur, with an ocean of glorious, majestic, virgin peaks comprised within the numerous well-defined ranges, snow-capped and glacier-scored, which tower above each other to new heights. There are rugged forest-clad slopes, flower-strewn passes, impressive solitudes, secluded fastnesses, charmingly beautiful lakes and tarns reposing in their mountain privacy like mirrors set in emerald, vast snow fields, turbulent torrents brawling down from the frozen torpitude of their glacial sources, and beautiful, sublime vistas of majestic summits, with wondrous, sweeping, spectacular panoramas where sunny valleys cleave the ranges of serrated, vapor-veiled peaks, all resolving into the subtle details of one harmonious whole.

There are four lines to take in such descriptive narrative, four parts of such scenes to play up,

or four themes to discourse upon. The first
three are emphasized most frequently; I believe
the last is the one by far the most important.

First, and oftenest spoken of, there is the health
giving climate. Here earth and air and sky and
water all combine, the forces of nature inanimate
conspiring to give of their best to induce new
health in human kind.

Secondly, there is the unrivaled beauty of scenery: nowhere else in the world is there a trip of the
same length more picturesque or one embracing
a greater variety of attractions than this from
Edmonton to the coast.

There is, thirdly, the historic interest attaching
to sights and scenes through which one passes.
For the place this region holds in American history
is second scarcely to that occupied by Plymouth
Rock and Jamestown. The events of the early
years here had the very romance of history and yet
they have not been the theme of historians. The
memories and traditions of those events are as
thrilling and romantic as of any in the volumes
of libraries and yet they have lain, for a century, mainly as matters of course and mere
statements of fact, in the files of the two rival

fur-trading companies—the Western and the Hudson Bay.

But, lastly, there is the inexpressible influence of the mountains upon one's emotions, the compulsion that they exercise upon one's moods. This is subtle, ethereal, evasive, and unreal: and yet it is most real; because it elevates, inspires, dignifies, and renders serious all who come under its spell. It is possible to tell tales of *coureurs du bois* until you make those actors long dead live again; it is possible to paint a picture with a pen, imprison color in a simile, pack melody in metaphors, and give a whiff of ozone in an illustration; but there are feelings that can only be discerned and not described; there are thrills of inspiration that cannot be passed along.

It is this that makes this region one in which to sit down calmly and invite your soul. Here is Nature, peaceful, pure, and undefiled, each one of these because the other. I have never seen a place so wild—nor one in which thoughts of great import were quite so easily caught.

And I said: If there's peace to be found in this world,
A soul that is humble might hope for it here.

CHAPTER X

Hectic Revels in a Far-off Land

N view of the relation assumed to exist between the efforts of the Church and the strivings of organized Labor in whatever makes for human betterment and in amelioration of conditions that tend toward degradation; because the Clergy are expected in their pulpits to speak messages of cheer or warning, in case of the former or the latter; for any or all of these reasons, it is fitting that space be devoted here to some study of types and conditions of men and communities of labor—and hard labor, too, at that.

But any one can speak words of advantage on this subject only from the vantage ground of personal experience; and he can do this with most freshness if he speaks from observations he has made most recently. My mind turns to a journey I have just completed—this last week in August—which has brought me here to Banff, as resting place, in the Canadian Rockies. It is worth depicting in a paragraph or two upon its own account and, in some others, too, because of some thoughts it stirs upon this special theme.

But, the journey itself? I am writing on too rapidly. The route was one of all but a full thousand miles. And yet it paid to take it, every mile of it: all of its dirt and danger, its discomforts and some dullness, its hard traveling and harder eating, its scant sleep and its travesty upon restful recreation. It will, one of these days, be a favorite trip for Eastern tourists. What has long been Mecca only for trappers, sportsmen, and anglers is yet destined to become one for the mountain climber and to be filled with resorts for those who seek all kinds of recreation. On the map it lies in the shape of a Pegasean horseshoe, the toe at Fort George, an old post of the Hudson Bay Fur Company, the two corks at the two Dominion national parks, one Jasper Park on the Grand Trunk Pacific, and the other at Banff Hot Springs, on the older, although still new, Canadian Pacific.

I had come up to Jasper from Edmonton. There I set out by rail through the Yellowhead

Pioneer Railroading in Northwestern Canada

Courtesy, Grand Trunk Pacific Co.

Pass, went as far as Tete Jaune Cache, and on
board a ballast train to Willow River. Thence,
by canoe outfit two days and a night, I paddled
with a guide way down the Fraser River to Prince
George. Here I took a steamer, still down the
Fraser, to Soda Creek, 155 miles and from there to
Ashcroft, a station on the main line of the C. P. R.,
360 miles west of Banff. That land trip is made
over a Government road, in an automobile stage,
163 miles.

The truth is, this scenery in British Columbia
has features that are all its own. Here are valleys
that are park-like. So wild and untouched they
are that they seem to be cultivated. I will
not consume space mentioning such commonplace
things as snow on the mountains in sight from the
valleys with their August climate; nor the atmosphere so rare that mountains forty miles off look
no farther, say, than four; nor the terminal moraines
of ancient glaciers removed with steam shovels to
make way for railroad sidings, wild and tumultuous
mountain tarns diverted into water tanks, the queer
green color of the glacial water and sulphur stalac-
tites and stalagmites in the caves of the hot springs.
We grew used to seeing clear, cold water gushing

out of solid rock and would not have been startled
to find, in scriptural phrase, "oil out of the stony
rock." These, albeit works of Nature, are the
works of Nature's God.

Yes, one would think so. But I recall with a
nightmare sort of memory those nightly revels in
the huts, log cabins, wickiups, and lean-tos, in the
camps of the construction gangs along the railroad's right of way. And, now I come to think
of it, this was the thing that I set out to write of,
after all. It was not scenery but "scenes" that
gave impressions. And those scenes were hectic:
those night revelries were nothing short of
hellish.

"End of Steel" is a movable station. It has
moved westward ever westward, as the grade was
fixed, the ties laid and the rails spiked to them, by
stages in sections; but it marked, stage after stage,
the startings and the stoppings, halting points and
staying places, of all who went with the railroad's
building. Scouts, surveyors, graders, and construction gangs, station men, telegraph corps, and
track layers—these were the fraternities that
brought up, all at one time, some time soon or late,
at one place of foregathering. I saw certain of these

places and the sights were such as demons would delight in.

Life is free here; but the freedom, alas, is the bad freedom of license; and those who indulge it soon become licentiate. There are appetites engendered, lusts indulged, and passions gratified in ways and to degrees that leave no stopping place, and from which there will be no turning back, this side the Day of Judgment. Sherman described war with as much accuracy as he phrased his description with brevity; yet his description would be quite as true and quite as graphic if applied to any "End of Steel" town in the mountain section of a new transcontinental railroad. Life in these camps is an orgy at night as wild as the labor by day is adventurous. There is no way of exaggerating the vice, the villainy, and victimizing in which its horrors have to be depicted. The three concomitants of all camp following abound and work their ravages, the same old trio of the Devil's agents—wine, women, and song.

I remember—it always will haunt me—the grave by the roadside up at Willow River, a few feet of earth rectangular, enclosed in a crude corral and its wooden cross embowered with spruce and

laurel. And yet I would rather be its lonely
occupant than one of the two dozen D. T.'s I saw
in the Snake Room at the Palace(!)Hotel down the
river. I remember McBride, town of mosquitoes
and gumbo mud, deserted since "them graders" left
it stranded like a ship high out of water in the Bay
of Fundy when the tide has gone off seaward; but
I would live here in preference to Fort Blank, which
had last winter, in a center of only two thousand
bona fide inhabitants, more than fifteen thousand
workmen tributary to its dives and dance halls.

Have you ever seen, or can you picture, a town
only of that size with twenty-eight saloons, a
hundred and fifty lewd women, and not an officer
in the town? Did you know that thirteen dead
men were found under the snow when the thaw
came late in the spring? Such is the story that
they tell of Taft, Montana, when the tunnel was
put through on the St. Paul Extension back in the
"old days of nineteen five." This road is not
exceptional! This story is but typical. It is all
dreadful, terrible, horrible! I suppose it is even
culpable, on somebody's part; but it is difficult
to see on whose. It is regrettable. Ah, more; it is
unspeakably lamentable! Perhaps it is avoidable.

If so, it is the task of every earnest soul to strive for such a reformation as will become reclamation. At present this is the price the Sons of Martha pay in order that the Sons of Mary may ride over a great railroad safely and in comfort.

CHAPTER XI

A Week in Glacier National Park

" WHEN you come to the end of a perfect day," is the day Sunday? Is it Lord's Day of this full midsummer, this first week of August? And is the place of discovery the Glacier National Park? I have come back to this mammoth entrance hotel from the mountains, where I have been close to nature for a week. Here to-day, in 2000 square miles of cathedral-domed, snow-sculptured, glacier-aisled, and rock-shrined territory, not a place of worship exists—save all places. There is not a sanctuary—save the million that have been builded and constructed by creative hands of Nature's God.

The day is the close, moreover, also of a perfect week. Arriving only Monday—how long ago it seems—we found ourselves, from two days' crossing of the prairies, at the very foot of the throne where God must have sat the day he made America.   Here are the new Alps of the Western World. Here is a wonderful tumbled region possessing sixty glaciers, 250 lakes, as many stately peaks, precipices 4000 feet high and valleys of a corresponding depth, all of astonishing and rugged beauty.   Here is scenery equaling any in the world.   Here are two hotels also, one at either entrance and, between them, Gunsight Trail across the high top of the range, the very ridgepole of the roof of the world.

This Park, be it said, is in farthest northwestern Montana.   It incloses more than 1500 square miles of mountain magnificence.   Its scenery is strikingly Alpine; yet it possesses individuality to a high degree.   In ruggedness and sheer grandeur it probably surpasses the Alps, although geologically it is markedly different.   Here the Rockies are wondrously sculptured by gigantic glaciers of the long ago.   They are gorgeously colored above timberline by strata of red, green, and yellow limestone.   Peaks quaintly named by the Blackfeet Indians rear their heads two miles above sea level, the whole region extending northward to the Canadian border, and westward to the Flathead River.   So much for geography, as for geology: now for descriptive narrative.

How far we were from home, at what a unique point we had arrived, how strikingly East and West here come face to face, how sharply Occident meets Orient, how here the frozen North and plain-swept South both overlap, and how the *Fin de Siècle* meets the very Ancient of Days, was well illustrated in the strange admixture at the entrance on arrival. For both natural and artificial features, both the works of Nature and of man in taming nature, combine to accentuate these contrasts.

We stepped surprisedly from out the train to be met by the sound of tomtoms beaten by a group of Blackfeet Indians, robed in bright blankets, sons of old-time chiefs since educated at Carlisle. Jin-rikishas from the hotel met passengers, which hotel had tall totem poles for ornaments. Within, the dining-room had Swiss-costumed waitresses who vied with Geisha girls acting as waitresses in the grill room. Outside, cowboys rode to and fro to herd the occupants of tents, while automobiles were prepared to take them touring. Bear-skin rugs, imitation cherry blossoms, Navajo rugs, and Chinese pagoda effects commingled in the decoration of the hotel entrance, where old Chief

Three Bears was engaged in making war-dance music which was drowned by the shrill bleating of a pianola. The sound of running water in a mountain torrent mingled with the chug of the gasoline engine off in the laundry. While, at a safe distance, but their caution disregarded by paleface intruders, a dozen Indian tepees squatted about the starting station of the Park Transportation Company's dust-defying, eighteen-passenger big auto buses for the journey mountainward and far away. Small wonder that we fled, that we returned only to-day, returned from seven wonderful days' travel through that rare land of enchantment? Here, arriving back to-night after a long journey from the heart of the region, is it any wonder that we feel we have come to the end of a perfect week?

Atop one of those auto-stages we went motoring among the Rockies. Aboard trim launches we cruised over mile-high lakes. On sturdy ponies, in the wake of companionable guides, we went a-horseback over forest trails that wound up and on top of the mountains. We started from this queer hotel, fashioned out of big timber, and came to small Swiss-patterned chalet-groups, built of logs and stone. We slept in India tepee camps, all hostelries in which the spirit of the out-of-doors has been brought under roof or canvas.

Far above timber line we glimpsed, caused by the work of yesterdays, bright active glaciers of the nowadays. There are nearly a hundred of these, Blackfeet, the greatest, boasting of five gleaming square miles. They are the great-grand-children of the Park's primeval icefields. Valley glaciers, bench glaciers, lateral moraines, terminal moraines, crevasses, ice caverns, streams milky with the rock flour of the glaciers' grinding—all these give legitimately its name "Glacier" to the Park.

We went over the lakes and rivers in swift, natty little steamers. How these ever came here, inland at such distance from their birthplace, is a mystery akin to that of whence the sea gulls come that fly above the waters of Salt Lake. We journeyed to, paused at, and camped beside Swiftcurrent and Piegan, Two Medicine and Going-to-the Sun, and all the other many ponds and peaks and passes. We approached and passed, through its high gates, that notch—the Continental Divide—seven thousand feet and

McDermott Lake from Many-Glacier Hotel

Courtesy of the Burlington Route

more above sea level. Beneath us, on one hand, the waters started journeying toward the Gulf and Hudson's Bay; beneath us, on the other hand, they started toward the nearer Pacific. All about us the Rockies spread and outspread, hundreds of square miles of them, where among glacier patches you may snowball in midsummer.

Yet here is a place where, to your heart's content, you may get into the woods. Through all the Park's valleys—form the V-shaped declivities of streams scoured by the ancient glaciers into graceful U-shaped amphitheaters—and up the mountainsides to timberline are splendid forests of fragrant pine and spruce and balsam. Everywhere also wild flowers carpet the floors of these forested valleys—wild flowers and berries and grasses of more than two hundred varieties. For, unlike the Yellowstone, this park is a veritable flower garden. There is bear grass—the root of which was used by the Indians for making "good medicine"—yellow adder's tongue, flowering dogwood, wild gentian, mountain lilies, forget-me-nots, larkspur and dozens of varieties of daisies and other wild flowers, beautiful because of their profusion. Could one worship in such rare

7

environs? One might as well ask the same question regarding the Garden of Eden.

Here is also a place where, to your heart's content, you may be on and about the water. Down from those melting glaciers mighty cataracts go tumbling to beget hurrying rivers, vivid green, sparkling and foaming. These rivers feed, some of them, mile-high lakes, and out of these lakes the rivers go scurrying down to the plains. The waters of those lakes are still waters mirroring the peaks which rise sheer from their shores. They are waters ideal for boating; while both in the lakes and in the rivers, if you are a fisherman, myriads of mountain trout await your rod.

As for game, it is so wild, so unmolested, that it is yet tame. Hunting is prohibited, of course, because the Park is a government game preserve. In consequence, all types of animals and birds of the Rockies are to be seen and admired, not slaughtered and slain; the bighorn sheep, a famous mountain climber; deer, both blacktail and whitetail; elk, moose, the high-flying ptarmigan, and the odd whistling marmot. Mink and marten exist in large numbers, and several colonies of beaver inhabit the streams. Great numbers of mountain sheep inhabit the steep slopes. In the valleys are elk in abundance, and we saw all sizes of both black and silver-tip and grizzly bear feeding in the huckleberry patches. Here is the one place alone in America where I have seen the snowy Rocky Mountain goat. Very many of these, day in and day out, along their own skyland trails, pick their nimble-footed way about the mountaintops, their exploits to be followed easily through our field glasses.

Thus came we, after lapse of seven days, to journey's ending. It was barely sundown when we came, returning to this hotel although after nine o'clock. For in this far northern latitude the sun is loath to set and moon and stars both are as tardy in their rising. It is early August, but a huge indoor campfire is burning. This is no place for the thin-skinned or pale-blooded, even in this summer weather. Hence, in winter it must be cold beyond all belief. The registering thermometer shows fifty-seven degrees below zero at times. Between this high date and that low there must be all known varieties of weather. As we passed I noticed how the horses moved in pairs and stood from force of habit head to tail and leaned with necks across each other's flanks, from reminiscence of last winter's weather—or is it anticipation of the next? And the dogs! They have hair coats so heavy you can scarcely find the dog.

In from such outdoors we came to this lobby. It is the length of a city square. The ceiling is as high as the tops of tall trees of the forest. The walls are all decorated with pelts and adorned with skulls to which the horns are still adherent. Everywhere is peace and gladness on the part of the four hundred tourists and, above all protest, rings in riotous abandon the loud laugh of little children. They are loitering in droves, evasive of the eyes of anxious parents and prolific of excuses why they should not go to bed. But in this they are unlike their elders. For this is a place to sleep. Hence, there be many who would find excuse instead to keep tryst with one Morpheus. The air has been provocative of somnolence and drowsy are the guests, top-booted, khaki-clad, sunburned, wind-beaten, and with appetite engendered by much walking and appeased not wisely, but too well. An open fire is burning, open on all sides and covered only by a chimney let down from the center of the ceiling in the manner of the time-approved wigwam. I am sleepy. And I must prepare to be off in the morning. But I have found and enjoyed a perfect week in a perfect place. I have "come to the end of a perfect day."

CHAPTER XII

Six Days by Stage in the Yellowstone

 HAVE just completed the six days' circular journey by stage through the Yellowstone National Park. I am moved to admiration, but still more to awe. Here, if one loves nature, he can see it in all its sublimity. Elsewhere he may seek his pleasure; here he will be sobered, rendered serious, even religious. For one cannot look upon these scenes unmoved. He cannot observe, as here, the very handiwork of the Creator in that evolution of earth's forces, caught, detected, exposed in the very process, without having his thoughts turned from nature up to nature's God.

For the most striking peculiarity of this whole region is the apparently unearthly aspect of it all. This begets in the observer a sort of weird, uncanny feeling. He realizes that he is in nature's workshop and that he is looking upon the process of the world's construction. The most curious thing

is that, even in the presence of such gigantic
forces, one has not the slightest sense of danger.
There is a strange temper of abandon that this
environment produces and there is a feeling of
elation it engenders.

Curious withal is the mixture of sights and
sounds. Here is a place where the universe appears to be topsy-turvy. There are drifts of snow
in summer. There are mountains at once snow
and verdure-clad. There are glaciers sloping
off abruptly from the very edge of steaming
craters. You may stand and gather flowers from
sunny plains and, raising your eyes, look off at
snow-clad mountains in the near foreground. You
may here do fearsome things and yet not be afraid.
You may have come to laugh or scoff; you will
remain to pray.

In mere matter of location, the Yellowstone
National Park is that portion of the northwest
corner of the State of Wyoming, fifty-five by sixty-
five miles square. It embraces an area of 3500
square miles, has an average elevation of about
8000 feet above sea level, and is encircled by
magnificent mountain ranges. It is certainly one
of the most delightful parts of the American con-

tinent. When it was set aside to be forever the grand tourist resort of the people, and their common property, few had any idea of the endless variety and stupendous grandeur of the features it contained; now it is visited yearly by myriads.

The drive around this six days' circuit covers a route of 147 miles, over a carefully constructed Government wagon road. No railroad or trolley line has ever been constructed, nor ever is to be, the only mode of transportation being the more picturesque one either by stage or on horseback. Even on the regulation coaches of the transportation companies one may take as long as he chooses, stopping off at each place as many days as he pleases and continuing, on his coupon ticket, when he is ready. Last Summer automobiles were admitted.

The stage route begins where the railroad ends, where over the entrance is fittingly inscribed: "The Gate to the Mountains." The route, through the Park and back again to the same entrance, is over the finest and most picturesque part of the Rocky Mountains, the whole at an altitude of about a mile and a half above the level of New York or Philadelphia, a height from which one might look down upon Mt. Washington, a quarter of a mile.

On this drive, continued thus six days, we passed through cañons and beneath crags, over mountains and through valleys. We stopped to drink from springs which are the heads of rivers. We traversed long slopes and smiling grass-carpeted and flower-bordered valleys. We passed in sight of petrified forests. At points every here and there we came suddenly out upon terraces where great wide panoramas opened of pine trees and snow-clad peaks all the way around the high horizon. And we constantly caught glimpses of the Three Tetons, mountains of Wyoming, triple symbols of eternity, one forty, one sixty, one a hundred miles away.

The first day's drive is from that Entrance Gateway to the Mammoth Hot Springs Hotel, the center of the first scene of interest, seven miles inside the boundary line. The whole region here is spoken of familiarly as "The Formation," since it consists of the boiling hot springs and their result-ing terraces. From the hotel one needs no guide to point direction to these, as the strong smell of sulphur and the brilliant coloring in the sunlight

serve to locate them.   They are so large indeed as
to be in themselves almost the sides of mountains
and, in their shape and coloring, although not
in their temperature, they resemble Niagara as
it would be frozen.   As one proceeds over the
sediment-encrusted coating separating these springs
from each other, he feels that only the thinnest
shell separates him from the very center of the
earth.   The springs, level full to the surface with
clear boiling water, are perfect pictures in color,
which color is due to deposits, the constituent
elements in solution being lime, arsenic, magnesia,
and sulphur.

The second day out is a drive of forty miles,
broken in the middle at noonday for two hours'
stop at the Norris Lunch Station.   The road to
this point winds through the Hoodoos, the Golden
Gate, and Silver Path to that large area of twenty
acres which looks like a field of petrified snow.
The sight of steam rising here from numerous
earth vents gives to the whole the appearance of
some great community of factories submerged;
while the sound emitted from earth crevices is
like the sound of the Mills of the Gods, all out of
sight.   Glimpses may be had here of places, so

In Yellowstone National Park

many of which have been named after him who is fittingly thought of as the Prince of this realm; as, for instance, the Devil's Cave, the Devil's Kitchen, the Devil's Frying Pan, etc. One of these, the Devil's Bathtub, is of such temperature as certainly only he himself, inured to his own special climate, would enjoy.

The inside of others of these caves resembles nothing else so much as that scene on the operatic stage where the Rhine-maidens swim in "Das Rheingold." The exterior of one is shaped like the grinning skull of a fiend who has committed suicide; while all about the others, deposits have been contorted into shapes resembling goblins and gargoyles. One of these in the distance is so large that it looks like the ruins of some great stone castle recently destroyed by fire, and, with its towers and battlements, perpetually smoking.

Another drive of twenty miles brought us for an overnight stop to the Fountain Hotel. Here is the region of those curious boiling springs of mud. Some, because of the presence of so much lime, are so white, and because of the fluidity of their substance so thick, that they look like great pots of boiling ice cream. Huge bubbles may be

seen in process of formation, forming so slowly
that it is easy to follow the actual process. The
chief of these is the Mammoth Paint Pot, a circular
disk the shape and size of the crater of some great
volcano. The liquid is composed of oil, water,
clay, and lime, and the result of the mixture is such
a perfect paint that the walls of the dining-room
here, having been coated with it seven years ago,
still preserve their color perfectly.

The third day's drive brought us to the region of
the geysers. These are springs of water which boil
and bubble normally level with the surface of the
ground, but which, at intervals, varying from once
an hour to once a week, erupt at heights ranging
from thirty to three hundred feet. When not in
eruption the water is so placid that one may approach directly to its edge and look down into the
holes, which extend no one knows how near to the
center of the earth. An eruption never leaves
the observer dissatisfied. Each of the geysers
does all that is advertised—does it never in haste
and always with great dignity. The explosions
performed, and the pressure of the heat below
which has generated this explosive force relieved,
the water subsides, the operation to be repeated

once again at the end of another interval, as it has perhaps for the past 50,000 years.

On the fourth day a drive of twenty-five miles during the forenoon brought us by noon to the Thumb Lunch Station, standing on a projection out in the lake. This lake is about thirty miles in width, and that distance we traversed on board a steamer which plies from this point to the Lake Hotel. During that forenoon we had crossed the famous Continental Divide, the highest point in the Park, or, for that matter, upon the American Continent. It extends north and south in an irregular line, thus forming the watershed for the streams flowing both ways, the one to the Pacific, the other eventually to the Atlantic Ocean.

This lake, with the accompanying region, is the point deepest in the forest from civilization and hence the place in which both game and fish the most abound. One has only to cast his line to catch trout, as many as he cares to count. It is at this Lake Hotel also that tourists are not only likely, as they are at the other hotels, but at this one certain to see, every evening after dinner, bears which have become accustomed to come down each evening out of the forest to feast on the gar-

bage thrown out from the kitchen. They are so
tame that they may be approached with impunity,
at least near enough to be photographed. That
night I counted fourteen in one group not fifty
yards from the hotel veranda.

The next day a short drive of ten miles brought
us to the Falls of the Yellowstone River. If height
of wall and depth of waterfall, if beauty of verdure
underfoot, and majesty of towering cliffs overhead,
if harmony and strength and wealth of beauty
constitute greatness, then these Falls are the finest
sight in all the world. Here is the point at which
the whole river plunges over a precipice, swiftly
at first in a narrow stream, then, a little lower,
seeming to go down a little slower. The rate,
instead of being accelerated, seems retarded, and
the whole spreads out into a graceful flowing sheet
of foam. The crest is a line of silver, its foam
reaching to the clouds in mist, while at its foot the
whole is circled as though with a girdle by a rainbow. Nothing can do justice to this scene. It is
one place that even guide-books cannot exaggerate.
Some have essayed description and have found some
small success as they came on from day to day
until they reached this climax at the Falls; but here

despair always seizes them. They give it up and throw their notes over the brink of the Canyon as one drops his flowers at the tomb of Napoleon.

On the sixth day, the drive continues from these Falls down the Canyon for six miles before it turns toward home. Those who have seen all the other leading features of the world's great natural phenomena, agree that here all seem to have been brought together and thrown over the edge of that chasm into that abyss in one glorious confusion and in one dissolving mixture of enchantment. Any adequate portrayal of this sight awaits the invention of some satisfactory method of color photography. There is the luster of pearl, jasper, opal, and amethyst in such abundance and confusion as to remind one of the place whose streets are proverbially paved with gold, whose walls are jasper, and whose gates are pearl. Here is a place so wonderful that, up from a part of earth so beautiful, one's thoughts turn of their own accord to Heaven.

CHAPTER XIII

Cody Road to Yellowstone Park

HE principal object of interest at the end of the new Cody Road into Yellowstone Park is—the Yellowstone Park. At the other end, there lies a region equally distinct—the ranch home country of one, William F. Cody, who to all the world is known as "Bill"—Buffalo Bill. The distance between these is one day's journey of eighty-six miles, which can now be made upon smooth-rolling big ten-passenger new auto busses. It was Sunday. We were traveling. Why should we not go on? Indeed, it was a model way to spend the day; for we saw sights and scenes symbolic of the great works both of God and man.

The family name of Cody will not exactly be immortalized by the town's hostelry, the Hotel Irma, named for the only daughter; but let that pass—like the sleepless night it gave us. There is soon a better to be builded. This one is a woeful example of how incompetent the management can be of a monopoly. There is nepotism in appointment, absentee ownership, indifferent attention, lack of all efficiency, and Western ignorance of Eastern requirements of what it takes to make a tourist even moderately comfortable. In fact, this whole town seems to be here only because it came along one day and, startled into awe by the surrounding scenery, stopped short and has stayed ever since. The scene about the city at close hand is one of isolation, not to say of desolation. Concrete pavements run with the same regularity as chalk marks on a tennis court. They lie as white and blazing in the sun and over earth as bare and solid, as dry and as unproductive.

But we left early this bleak, sun-baked, almost sheepless sheep-ranch country, and passed westward from the city, with its 1500 stranded population and its sulphur mills adjoining it as touches in a picture of Inferno. Five miles out, on glancing back, we were not only glad that we had left it, but that we had this far sight of it. For we saw the whole town standing out, clear in the opalescent sunlight. We beheld it, through the early ambient air, looking like nothing so much as a

8

mirage on the desert. Thus it became no longer a nightmare, but a dream; a fading recollection of a place unreal; a passing point of pilgrimage for guests who had but tarried for a night.

We were fortunate in three particulars, in the kind of a day we happened upon, in the personnel of our mixed company, and in our chauffeur, guide, philosopher, and friend—and all in equal quantities—one Frank O. Thompson. Although cautious at the wheel, away from it he was communicative and informative. He even made the time pass quickly across the first stretch of common or garden variety of sagebrush scenery by tales of early-day pioneer and cowboy experience. The doctor, who was from St. Louis, started introductions; the school teachers from Duluth were willing to make known their names; the octogenarian became fairly playful; the heiress gave up her suspicion; the blasé curio collector from New York became communicative, the two college students dropped their *savoir faire*, and the Scotchman warned the company to have a care; for

There's a child amang ye takin' notes;
And, faith, he'll print 'em.

We had hardly time to size up our companions before reaching, five miles out, Shoshone Canyon, where enthusiasm broke down all restraint and prompted intimacy. From that point on converse sounded like a quilting party. I have never known such universal approbation of a day's adventure; nor have I ever seen sights that could merit it so well. For, picture the strange region as a whole. It is a region of large distances, of gigantic mountain peaks and ranges, green-sloped and snow-capped, heaped close together, apparently in inextricable confusion; while, over all this wildness, there is a soft and picturesque beauty.

Through Shoshone Canyon, this Cody Road has been chiseled in and through the rock, traversing as many as five tunnels in less than a mile. In some places it is so high above the river that the sound of the rushing water cannot be heard. Where there was once only a pioneer's trail, blazed through a forest primeval, there is now this special highway builded to accommodate the automobile public. Once, here was only a blazed trail for pack trains; now, the road is as carefully constructed as though for a trolley line. The grade rises from an altitude of 5000 feet at Cody to

8000 feet at the Lake Hotel, in the Park.   Between these points, still higher, it crosses the Continental Divide.

That cañon in particular is formed by the almost perpendicular sides of mountains rising above the river.   They are rocky, jagged, and barren of vegetation.   Through this is blasted from the native rock this solid highway.   Following the river, now level with it, now overlooking it from sheer, giddy heights, but always gradually rising, we finally reached a point above the top of the Government Dam.   Beyond and between the highway, ranges to the north and south gradually drew closely together.   Thence we took our winding way through mountains along which the Shoshone River and this Cody Road keep such close company for miles on miles.   We rode until, looking out westward, the road seemed barred by the Absaroka Range, apparently a solid mass from north to south, with forty snow-capped peaks, none less than 10,000 feet, and many reaching 12,000 feet.   The five-mile posts are conveniently placed to mark off stages of this quick kaleidoscopic journey to the entrance of the Park itself.   There one-mile posts began, whence twenty-six miles more remained to the Lake Hotel. We had time left after dinner to go on by private automobile to the new Canyon Hotel. That seventeen miles more than the prescribed eighty-six made in all about a century run—the most wonderful one hundred miles in America.

We passed at the outset the Shoshone Dam of the Government reclamation project, built at a cost of four and one-half million dollars to date and likely yet to cost three millions more. Already it reclaims waste land, a hundred and thirty-two thousand acres of it. And there is possibility of three hundred full thousand more. It is a body of water comparing with a boy's idea of a mill-dam about as a giant's bathtub compares with a thimble. For this reservoir—this lake—is forty-two miles in circumference. The Dam itself is the highest in the world, three hundred and twenty-eight feet at its face, thirty-seven feet higher than the Flat-iron Building; yet below and beside this it is im-bedded eighty feet in the hard granite underneath and extends laterally into the like solid granite mountains sixty feet on either side.

We left Cedar and Rattlesnake Mountains standing so high in an atmosphere so clear that they were not to disappear for twenty-five miles. Through the Dude Ranch Country there were some irrigated stretches; but at the end of this we left the last fence we were to see for fifty miles. Two tall peaks narrowed in the passage here and upon either side, high as the clouds, were planted waving flags marking the edge of the National Forest Reserve. Up the long tortuous valley of the North Fork we proceeded, coming at Pahaska Tepee to the lunch station. Pahaska is Sioux, meaning "long hair." It is an Indian tribute of affection to Colonel Cody; for the place was named for this prince of guides and trappers, scout and hunter, aborigine father and friend.

On up the river we passed, to the Soldiers' Station at the eastern entrance of the Park. Up and over Corkscrew Bridge we went, rounded the Double S bend, and came to where snow still lay in Sylvan Pass. Here tales were told how, at the end of June, when they shoveled out the road, it was thirty feet deep. All decamped to go snow-balling—this in August. But small wonder, when one realizes that the altitude is 8760 feet. Sylvan Lake is twenty miles from journey's ending. But, passing the Apollonaris Springs and Iron Springs,

In Shoshone Canyon on the Cody Road

Courtesy of the Burlington Route

bubbling, smoking, turbulent "Formations," we were apprised we were approaching Land of Wonders; and our expectations were not raised too high. For we came into the shadow of tall snow-capped sleeping mountains and soon were in sight of the Three Tetons. Passing Mirror Lake, we threaded the Basins—and always we had for company those far hills, snow embosomed.

Upon that journey we had passed strange wonders beyond compute or compare. We had climbed up grades as steep as stairways and as crooked as a spiral for five miles upon a stretch. We had noted, way back at the outset, the curious stratification of rocks—granite superimposed upon sand and shale. We had ridden past and underneath huge hanging rocks. We had loosed brakes and run face-on against cliffs of a thousand feet piled on a thousand feet. We struck long, perfectly straight stretches, where the only curves were undulations and the only motion up and down. We fled over this smooth roadway, swooping in such manner as to give one the sensation of a dip-the-dips or shoot-the-chutes. Bare mountain rock masses arose, hovered, and sank out of sight. Rocks stood as sheer and straight as castle walls, beyond and past the point where the road creeps under the edge of Thousand Foot Cliff. There were miles on miles of mountain timber interspersed with grassy slopes, but there was never a dead tree in all that distance. Those are the tallest, steepest, and still timbered mountains I have ever seen.

We saw game and fish and birds and flowers, and all these in abundance. There were beaver dams. We counted in one band two hundred elk. Along the road we found deer calmly feeding. Only ten miles out from Lake Hotel, we saw a moose. Later, we came to the lake itself, that true fisherman's paradise. On tall peaks there were nesting places for eagles. And the bird itself was oft in evidence. It had not yet learned that it ought to be seen rather than heard; for we learned repeatedly, and by experience, the meaning of "the eagle's scream."

In that early region of wonders akin to the grotesque, the sublime, the ridiculous, the uncanny, and the supernatural at once, it required but little imagination to see the red rocks take on any semblance the guide pointed out. There were, for example, the Sleeping Giant, the Dead Indian, the Clock Tower, Pinnacle Point, Statuary Hill,

Chimney Rock—thus on and on *ad infinitum.*
These began with the Holy City; they reached
their climax at Wapiti. Between these points
were thirty miles of red stone monuments, towers,
minarets, gargoyles and semblances and shapes too
many for depiction. In the Holy City itself there
were buildings high as castles, piled on top of tall
sky-scrapers, and these having pyramids for
the foundations. Yonder was a shaft as tall as the
Washington Monument, there a span long as the
Brooklyn Bridge, while on top of each a stretch
of verdure grew as green and brilliant as the
shingles on a painted roof.

Nothing was more striking upon this whole
journey than the extreme degrees of brilliancy and
contrast of sharp tints of color. The mountains,
back at the beginning, were not snow-clad, but
they were as white as snow, because of their peculiar structure. These gave way to yellow, those
in turn to that peculiar brown familiar to the
patrons of the movies when the scenes are laid in
Colorado. All the sands were as brown as the
trees were green, and the flowers were as blue as
the long mounds of iron-ore clay were so bril-
liantly red. Sandrock gave way to granite, yellow

changed again to brown, and colors multiplied, bright, native, virgin, and unsullied. Whiles, adorning all these, were the fields of flowers— fields, gardens, and bouquets of them.

This Cody Road has almost all the features of all the famous sight-seeing places combined in this country. It has features severally grander than their greatest ones in series. The Shoshone Canyon, through the bottom of which we rode, is as deep as the Yellowstone Canyon, from the brink of which later we looked down. The snow-capped mountains all about us, although at a distance, were impressive as the Selkirk Range on the Canadian Pacific. The Falls of the Yellowstone are as fine as Niagara. Frost's Caves, under Cedar Mountain, are as extensive as those in Kentucky. The approach to Absaroka Range is between rock walls as narrow, looking up to peaks quite as precipitous, as in and through the Royal Gorge on the Denver and Rio Grande. The Corkscrew is like that at Georgetown, Colorado; while those miles of brownstone pinnacles beat Manitou and all the Garden of the Gods at their own game. And, as for Wild West country, it is that about the town of Cody, surely a whole county being Buffalo Bill's winter quarters for himself and his mixed company.

Whichever way you travel, you will wish to return by the same route in the other direction. Beginning with Shoshone Dam and ending over Sylvan Pass, whichever way you go you reach a climax at the other end. The Dam, adown that former Canyon, was the work of man; the Canyon of the Yellowstone is the lone work of Nature, untouched by the hand of man. In one place, there is more that is natural than artificial; in the other case, all things are *vice versa*. Here is nature; there, man's ingenuity in overcoming nature. The difference is in this: that, whereas there we had a feeling of pride in achievement of our kind, here we were awed into humility at sight of something so sublime it could be carven only by the hand of God.

I never have enjoyed a single day's journey so much in my life. And such was the composite verdict of our complex company. If enthusiasm waned at any point, it was only because of multiplicity of wonders; for we rode entranced until new marvels by the mile grew commonplace. The sustained beauty and grandeur of this scenery is greater than within the Park itself.   And yet this Road is so new people scarcely know that it exists. The truth about it writes like fiction and the simplest facts read like romance.   This Cody Road is fitting monument to the memory of him whose name it bears, to Colonel Cody, who plans to be buried on the top of Cedar Mountain.

CHAPTER XIV

Estes National Rocky Mountain Park

THIS chapter is depiction of another summer Sunday's journey. It stands well in order of climax also; since among the places technically called "National" Parks—those districts set apart by Government enactment for the preservation of wild game, wild life, wild forests, and wild scenery —this is the latest, and perhaps the last: I mean the Estes Rocky Mountain Park in Colorado.

For many years, the Mecca of Eastern mountain lovers has been the Rockies. Yet it was not until one year ago that a particular section of that enormous scenic range was formally chosen as representative of the noblest qualities of the whole. This region, set apart by Act of Congress, September 4, 1915, includes about thirty miles of that great mountain chain. And well does it deserve the honor; for, from Panama to the Arctic Seas, the Rockies have no spot comparable to this, both for wild, rugged glory and for velvet park-like beauty.

Time also was when the trip to this region was an adventure; to-day the entire region is at Denver's very gate. For many years those lofty peaks had been accessible, on foot and horseback, but by labored stages; within the past year automobile roads have been built. The favorite line of approach is the new road, in from Loveland Station, on the Colorado and Southern Railroad.

This town of Loveland seemed rightly named that early morning, as we came to it across the lovely garden-country that surrounds it, level as a lawn, productive beyond measure, place of orchids, ranches, fields, and farms, all irrigated, all bearing the veritable burden of their harvest. Boarding one of the huge auto busses that awaited the train's coming, we were soon away on the ride and climb that were to take us across the broad valley, up the steep ascent.

The plains lay off to the east; while, straight to the west, was the crest of the continent, snowy white and towering above our heads. Seven miles across the lowland, and we entered the cañon of the Big Thompson River. We were to emerge, twenty-five miles farther up, at Estes

Park. That road is a steady ascent, as consistent but as sinuous, as the river itself. Seventeen times it crosses from one side to the other of the cañon to make way for the waters which rage and toss and tumble in rapids, in filmy waterfalls, in seething torrents of white whirlpools, ever battling their way through the rocks to the valley below.

As the course narrows, its attractiveness expands. The car hugs the left wall, beneath dizzy, pine-clad heights. On the right is a yawning gulch, where at times the stream is hidden beneath confused masses of rocks. But ever it appears and reappears, foaming, boiling, clamoring, rioting, until anon parks open and pictures form themselves and re-form like dissolving views. Here and there swift dashing creeks would cross the roadway, like some frightened animal, and turn back in gulches below to roar like the same animal at bay; for the mountain tarns here are as wild as the wild game really is tame.

Valleys opened out, then sides of mountains closed us in. Streams came straight down over sides so steep that, in their spilling, they looked like the waters from a broken rain-spout. Off steepest mountainsides of solid granite, water would start from the melting snow-banks at the top to end by irrigating patches of wild flowers in valleys underneath. The verdured hills would shrink back and leave the bleak peaks towering monuments. Green trees deserted the landscape, as we ascended, and groups of aspens began to shiver in the breeze.

Quaint beauties, grotesque shapes, and strange illusions crowded the way also. One of the most striking of these was the apparent phenomenon of water flowing uphill because of the continuous upgrade of the road. And the trees! Especially those aspens! Their white trunks and branches matched the luxuriance of their bright foliage. The roads led here and there through rows of them that stood as straight and white as do the pillars in a marble hall. Off on the heights, eleven thousand feet up, the winter's struggles between trees and icy gales were grotesquely exhibited. We were in sight of that strange region of clouds and storms where the barometer often stands at seventeen inches, they say, and where water boils at 184 degrees Fahrenheit. Is it any wonder that the human body and the human mind, in presence of such new conditions, manifest new feelings?

This road as an auto road has not had its second annual birthday; but tin cans strewn along the way show what it had been formerly—a wagon road for camping parties. Since its christening, more recent tokens bespeak admiration at chief points of interest and show where parties have paused in their passing. Candy boxes, here and there a hairpin, now a blown veil, then a strayed straw hat, but chiefly paper covers torn from rolls of kodak films, bestrew the spots where parties have paused and dismounted and where interest has focused cameras. These are marks of practical appreciation by those who foregathered at these points for rhapsody.

We met and passed all kinds of parties, some but lightly laden, some with wraps and baggage quite enough to cross the ocean. And these latter, the children of this world, were wiser in their generation than the former, the children of light; for it is overcoat weather here even in August. There were camping flats and on them camping parties. There were wagon trains and there were pack trains. There were tourists roughing it *de luxe*,

9

and there were those who took their pleasures roughly. There were campers with mixed out-fits of all grades of luxury and penury. There were prairie schooners, vestiges of a picturesque past; and there were new sheep-herders' wagons, with all up-to-date equipment.

One of the things most noticeable was the amount and the variety of camp and cottage, tent and other kinds of outdoor life along the way. Next after the number of automobile parties mov-ing up and down the long tortuous valley, with precarious turns and sudden stops and starts, were the hundreds of places where people had stopped —not to care when they started again. It is hard to catch the spirit of this outdoor life, unless you happen to have taken that same spirit with you. Just to be alive in the eloquent and ever-changing presence of those carved and tinted peaks is in itself a satisfaction.

We brought up at the end of three hours at Estes Park proper, a valley village of many hotels. The surprising thing here is that all things are so new. It is surely up to date in every possible particular. There are traffic regulations and a bonded indebtedness, antiseptic drinking foun-

Mountain-Surrounded Village of Estes Park

Courtesy of the Burlington Route

tains and a fire department, a high school and a motion-picture palace, churches and manicure parlors—and garages. For the automobile has replaced the donkey, the chauffeur the cowboy, and the omnipresent Ford the bucking bronco. This village has about five hundred permanent residents, most of whom care for the comfort and pleasure of the hundred thousand tourists who are visiting the Park this summer.

I had been three times before across the State, but I had failed—as many travelers feel they fail —to see the things most heralded; the scenery and sports depicted in the old-time stereoscopic views, the modern movies, and the omnipresent railroad folder literature advising one to spend vacations in mountain-embattled, wind-swept, carefree Colorado. I had seen Pike's Peak? Yes. Colorado Springs? Of course. Denver? Just like any other modern city. But the snow-capped ranges, the mountains to be climbed, trails to be followed, fish to be caught, burros to be ridden, clean camps, clear air and crystal water, moonlight glades and cool October days in hot mid-August? They are all here. They are all to be seen, rolled and combined in one composite photograph. They are all to be felt in one well-ordered week's experience.

The Rocky Mountains are as well named as the Black Hills in Wyoming, the White Mountains in New Hampshire, or the Green ones in Vermont, the Bad Lands of Dakota, the Great American Desert, Lovers' Lanes, or Soldiers' Monuments—simply because they are so.   They are piles, masses and confusions of bare, solid rocks.   This part, however, is unique and without replica.   Here is the inspiration of the Creator's rarest moods.   Off yonder, vales lie at the foot of grim, scarred peaks; for they are fairly ramparted with walls of rugged mountains.   They are encircled by gigantic crooked arms, flung out from the main range; while below there are carpets of wild flowers and native grasses, shaded with pines and quaking aspens, stirred by the cool breezes from the snow-banks of the Great Divide.

The snowy portion of the range lies, roughly speaking, north and south.   Seen from this east-side village the peaks rise, in daring relief, craggy in outline, snow-mantled, awe-inspiring.   Midway and standing boldly forward from the western side, Long's Peak, 14,255 feet, rears his lofty, square-crowned head, a veritable king of mountains. In nobility, in calm dignity, in the sheer glory of stalwart beauty, there is no group to excel that company of snow-capped veterans of all the ages which stand at everlasting parade behind that grim helmeted captain. They are all glacial in their contour. For, indeed, one feature of this region is the readability of its records of glacial action during the ages when the world was making. Here is a veritable primer of geology, whose simple self-evident lessons disclose the key to Nature's chiefest secret. One might easily imagine places here to be the scenes of some titanic building project, the materials all assembled, but construction abandoned. Oblivion veils the mystic past. No crumbling parchments hint those thrilling tales. Yet they are older than all religions that are thus gazetted. Men may have lived and wrought and vanished in that long ago. If so, those great white mountains watched it all, then locked the secret in their mighty breasts. Here, where infinitude is so vividly portrayed, even one who elsewhere knows not reverence will bow his head.

But what is there to do? Most are content just to do nothing. The summits and the gorges, of course, resolve themselves into a choice between foot and horseback, if one wishes to explore. Or the sportsman may hunt and fish in the wildest of spots. But chiefly the worn-out city cliff-dweller loafs or rambles quietly around. He lets the more energetic ride and drive, climb mountains or play golf or tennis or work hard at resting. Here is a place merely to lie supine and rest; to listen to the voices of the swaying forests, the music of those limpid, purling streams, to gaze on a world of color, to feast on Nature's graces, to breathe God's purest air, and to offer thanksgiving to Him for all He has bestowed.

But my allotted time is up. I have spent a week here and must go out to-morrow morning. And come we now to that morrow. It is Sunday. In spite of pseudo desecration by the touring parties traveling regardless, still a sort of Sunday silence prevails, a kind of proverbial Sabbath-day calm. Even to the commonplace man, this trip down and out is like a chapter from one of Jules Verne's romances. He meets no antediluvian monsters, to be sure; but he passes scenes where these can easily be imagined. Whatever susceptibility to grand impressions, whatever poetic fancies the dullest minds may have, they are sure to be aroused by this experience.

The scenic changes from the majestic grandeur of the mountains to the pastoral beauty of the plains are sudden and surprising. Different was the scenery at every turn of the serpentine trail. There, to the west, stood a thousand towering peaks in spotless white, majestic, beautiful, awful, while off to the east, a mighty ocean of plain, superb and placid, stretched, to all appearance infinite. We came straight out of the mountains on acres by the million of gently rolling prairie meadow, through which silvery rivers snake their way from the deep cañons above to fill the great irrigating ditches of fertile northern Colorado.

We had climbed up elsewhere just a week ago. Now we rolled down, always down, and by this other route. We had come up the short side, thirty-two miles of a right-angle triangle of which the railway line was the base; down the hypothenuse we went, twice thirty-five miles, on to Denver. We went down those lines and round those curves with all brakes off and knowing no speed limit. We had scarcely time to see the ever-changing scenery and ever-shifting scenes. In twenty miles we dropped in altitude 2000 feet, and came into the center of a region which the United States Department of Agriculture has declared to be the best in the world as to climate and soil. And this is flanked by precious and rare metal mining districts. This region has passed through many early vicissitudes; but now an empire lies within the shade of that tall portion of the Rocky Mountains.

CHAPTER XV

The Royal Gorge of Colorado

 STRANGE experience I have had lately makes appealing to me one group of a greater coterie—I mean the Laboring Class—I have had opportunity to observe closely in a quite peculiar way: the great fraternity of railroad employees as I have lived with them, ridden with them, and talked with them on a trip to and fro across the continent.

As it happens, I am a clergyman. By that same token I should sympathize with all who are down-trodden or oppressed or overworked. As it happens, however, I am not one of those who believe that the average workingman in this country is overworked. I decline to sympathize here without one eye on the facts. I am satisfied that the mass of working people do not work as hard as do some others in the professions instead. I am quite sure some of them work fewer hours and draw more wages than what serves the semblance of work on their part deserves.

And yet, labor as a class, has recognition. As a cult, it has its creed. And, for its future, it has its own prophets and its prophecies. This calls for compliment; it also calls for criticism. The very thing I most lament is that it is so distinctive a class. It is questionable whether it has loyalty to much outside itself. It is lamentable when the Church, the State, the Family, all as institutions, have to take subordinate positions to the Union.

But there is one type of laborers who deserve foremost recognition. I am thinking of the railroad men throughout the country. And I think in terms specific, because of much experience I have had during six weeks past upon a journey far across the Continent. I came out over one of what were originally the historic overland stage-roads but is now a railroad. Every mile has its own story of pioneer bravery, of heroism, of hairbreadth escape from hostile Indians, or fortuitous deliverance from storm or disaster. And every mile to-day has likewise its presiding genius and its guardians in overalls.

I am not of those, I say, who sentimentalize

over the poor, down-trodden, oppressed, grievance-
possessed and sympathy-deserving laboring man;
over Labor, punctuated with an exclamation point,
capitalized—and unionized.   My opinion, based on
a wide observation, is that he is usually over- rather
than under-paid.   My conviction is that he is un-
industrious and unambitious in this country as
compared with his foreign, his European, proto-
type.   My fear is that his cause is worst served
by many well-meaning but uninformed persons,
clergy, women, Socialists, and sociologists, and by
some only semi-sensible reformers, who take for
truth a lot of glaring falsities and gross exaggera-
tions shouted by a too familiar type, out in the
far West certainly, of I-Won't-Work exciters and
inciters, agitators, anarchists, *et cetera*.   In short,
I think his enemy and not his friend is the professional, paid, pseudo Labor Leader.

But, apart from this, in a class by themselves
and forming a guild of their own—all uninten-
tionally, perhaps, just by their own efficiency,
proficiency, industry, and effectiveness, reliability
and proven worth to bear responsibility, their
sense of duty most of all in guarding and safeguard-
ing so great a trust as human lives committed to

their care—there are the railroad employees in general and in particular that chosen minor guild of them, the crews, brakemen, conductors, firemen, flagmen, engineers, of passenger trains on those long transcontinental journeys.

I appreciate the care taken of passengers, as the result of which there are so seldom accidents. And I applaud the fine morale, the sobriety, and the efficiency of railroad employees above almost all other classes of laboring men. Behind these, and before them, *i. e.*, these employees, underneath them and above them, are the men who built these railroads and the minor and major officials both who operate them and who keep their manifold and complex workings in such smooth simplicity.

It was Mark Hopkins who once said: "I never see a locomotive without wanting to take off my hat to it." I have always felt the same way. But more, in the case of these great Western railways, in view of the romance of their building and the monster size they have attained, I have tried to estimate the toil involved in their construction and the genius necessary for their operation. For the railroad as an institution is, of all things else, a thing of power. Most people do not realize this fully, just as it is customary to take every commonplace thing for granted. Railroads are so ubiquitous to-day that their absence rather than their presence is considered remarkable. But, in their knowledge of and command over the forces of nature, the men who built them put the legends of mythology to shame. They have outdone the Gods of Olympus in harnessing the elements to do their bidding. They have emulated Prometheus in stealing the fire from the Altar of Zeus. They have outdone Joshua in causing the very sun to stand still in the heavens while they have reduced the time of transit between points upon the schedules hour by hour. The railroads are the enemies of sectionalism and the chief agents in democracy. Especially is all this true out here where these mighty transcontinental railways, with their 57,000 miles of lines, have bridged magnificent distances, have abolished the wilderness, are sweeping the great American desert off the map, and are drawing the valleys of the Columbia and the Sacramento into the circle of the world's activities and interests.

Recalling my rides over some of these roads, I

have a confused recollection of a series of perfectly clear-at-the-time impressions. I can still see in my dreams hand-cars whipped off the track to allow us to pass and freight trains run on sidings at our swift approach. I still visualize section gangs at their work and recall their wavings in greeting as we rolled by them. I remember the sensation of crossing high bridges and the mile-long spans of trestles. I remember long straightaway lines that seemed interminable and far flights across ravines that gave every sensation of a ride in an aeroplane. I made notes while the engine jostled them so badly that they are almost illegible. But, in their order, they grew in ascending series of sheer admiration for the men who make these wheels go round.

Of course, I am not writing railroad-folder literature and so I must not use the language of the advertiser; but I am moved to applaud one system over which I rode all day but recently, not so much for its marvelous scenery as for the almost unbelievable engineering feats that have made its construction possible. The "scenery" is so nearly perpendicular that what one needs for observation purposes would be a glass-topped car,

as in the far South Seas one requires a glass-
bottomed boat.   Everywhere were works of nature;
but here still more there was evidence of man's
triumph over nature.

What I mean is that yesterday I rode from Glenwood Springs to Colorado Springs, adown the
Canyon of the Arkansas and through the Royal
Gorge.   Each route out here has its distinctive kind
of mountain scenery.   The Canadian Pacific runs
around the mountains; the Northern Pacific runs
over the Rockies; the Denver and Rio Grande
runs literally through them.   We rode through
narrow gorges with sheer precipitous sides and
over brief expansive basins flat as ball-room floors,
with mountain-like walls of gigantic amphitheaters a dozen miles away.   We passed in review
great giant cliffs, yet almost never were we out of
sight or sound of tumbling, foaming water.

Which does not mean, however, we did not
climb mountain grades.   Here is the highest
crossing and here are the most massive mountains
in the United States.   It took a 317-ton Mallet
type, and in addition two huge Mogul locomo-
tives, to draw our train of fifteen cars.   At many
points the space is so narrow that even where there

is a double-track road the two tracks have to run the one on each side of the tumbling stream.

One is amazed that such a vast amount of sight-seeing is encompassed in so small a spot. But, still more, he is constantly amazed that it has been made accessible. Of the mountains, there are some gray, some white, some blue, some green; for they are bare, and snow and tree and verdure clad alternately. At point after point it is impossible to tell where the mountains stop and the clouds begin. Then lastly, we came as by way of climax to the Royal Gorge, the place that has had its picture taken oftener than any movie actress, and which looks more like its picture than a photoed popular baseball player.

The Royal Gorge is a gigantic chasm, in the heart of the mountains, cut from the summits of lofty peaks to their very foundation stones. Farther and still farther did we penetrate and, as we did so, the cañon became narrower and the massive walls rose higher until, in the center, the gorge is only thirty feet wide, while the walls rise 2627 feet above the track. At this point there is not sufficient room for the railroad and the river to run side by side; hence it was necessary to build the famous Hanging Bridge, which is suspended parallel with the river by immense steel supporters buried in the granite walls on either side. This was the first railroad that ever penetrated the Rocky Mountain fastness. Even to-day here is a dozen-mile panorama of marvels that beggar description. At Hanging Bridge the rugged rock cliffs, enclosing the roaring river and the track, rise so abruptly in mid-air for half a mile that they shut out the day and cause stars to shine even while the sun is high in heaven.

Between Salt Lake City and Denver, but more especially from Glenwood Springs to Colorado Springs, there lies this region famed throughout the world for scenic marvels and for feats of engineering skill. But more exceptional even than this route I took was the way I found of traveling in novel fashion; that is, with an engine permit. Being privileged beyond my wont, and for this once beyond my fellows, I occupied the elbow-leaning window by the fireman's seat high in the engine's cab.

Puffing and tugging the engine hauls its long train body upward until, through a tunnel at the

10

crest of the Tennessee Pass, 10,240 feet aloft, the
Pacific slope is changed for the Atlantic.   From
here, the passengers clutching like boys riding
on a bobsled, the train slides down the eastern
side of the Rockies.   Immediately on the north is
Mount Massive, 14,424 feet, the highest peak in
the State, where we pulled into Gunnison station,
both the town and the river commemorating the
name of the captain of army engineers killed
hereabouts by the Indians in 1853.

The Grand Canyon, through which the Arkansas
pours from the high country to the lower, is ten
miles long, and the railroad, by a marvel of engineering enterprise and dint of much blasting and
ballasting, has made of it a thoroughfare renowned
the world over.   We slid, clinging close to every
twist and turn where there is scarcely space be-
twixt wall and river for the single track.   The
narrowest portion of the passage is the wondrous
Royal Gorge.   Here the red granite and gneiss
walls, sparkling with mica, tower aloft.   The sky
is a thread almost obliterated by the jagged
ramparts.   The river boils madly through.   The
engine sways now to the right, now to the left,
dragging the train.   The vista ahead, momentarily

blocked, opens again and in some unexpected manner a way is eventually found.

Now, when one makes such a journey, not by any means the least important of the things he learns and the new impressions he receives is a new and great respect for the railroads of his country; both for the railroad as an institution and for railroading as an occupation. On a journey such as this, after seeing any such road in all its parts and such a system in all its workings, one decides that more wonderful even, if possible, than the country that these roads traverse is the human genius, which in fifty years has shortened the journey across the continent from five months to as many days, and the still greater genius which, coupled with faithfulness and fidelity, have made that rate of speed commensurate with safety.

The fact is, railroad men themselves have no conception of the way in which those outside of their circle look upon both them and their business. To us the whole business of railroading is mysterious and the whole fraternity of railroad men are masters. I know of nothing else except this almost uncanny fascination which can explain how it is that railroads get into their service, oftentimes for relatively small pay, such relatively good men. But certain it is that, ever since the Civil War, railroading as a career has been more attractive to the bold and enterprising men and to the ambitious youth of America than any other occupation.

Is it possibly for this reason? Every man in the service of a railroad has something, whether it be a uniform, a cap, a flag, a brake bar, an oil can, a ticket punch, or what not, which gives him the distinction of a definite place, which marks him as a member with a rank in a company and which makes him of indispensable importance. He does something in some place which nobody else can do quite so well, and he does it in the eyes of a populace who to-day esteem his form of labor as one of special dignity. As Homer makes Ulysses say: "I would rather be a keeper of swine in the land of the mortals, than a king in the realm of shades," so it is that the young men of to-day are fascinated by, and attracted to, that form of labor in which they have this distinction more than in any other.

The total number of employees of this class in the United States is at present about a million. It is they who have changed railroading from an occupation into a profession. At the top, it is a highly complex profession; at the bottom, there is hard, but always highly skilled, labor. Between the two, no other calling has kinds of work so exacting. Only long and faithful service, a strictly first-class moral character, and undoubted ability to perform the duties of the position next above will insure any sort of promotion. The fact is that nowhere else in the world is promotion bound to be merited as it is among them. They all, in the nature of their occupation, had to begin at the bottom of some ladder and have reached or are reaching the top, if at all, only because they have more ability, character, and physical strength than their fellows. There is no other field in which it is so nearly impossible for square men to get into round holes.

My thought goes off at this moment to those poor devils, who are climbing at the risk of their lives over the tops of box-cars to obey the signals shrieked from locomotive whistles through the darkness; to those others who, with an application to duty fit to drive men insane, are working in signal towers and train dispatchers' offices; to those who, in loneliness akin to banishment, are track-walking on the mountains or telegraph operating on the prairies; to those who drive snow plows in the wilds of far Montana in the winter, or who work mud-dredges and pile-drivers in the Southern swamps; aye, even to the widows left desolate of the martyrs to their duty who frequently suffer fatal accident. But, even so, I reflect this is the price of progress.

With a clang and roll each new creation
Breaks forth 'mid blood and tears and tribulation.

The pathfinders, who blazed out this trail; the scouts, reconnoiterers, surveyors, and construction gangs, who gave it being; the contractors all and laborers; the firemen, linemen, roundhouse keepers, and track-walkers; the telegraphers and switchmen; the men who have made this railroad and now make the wheels go round—they are true pioneers of empire, these begrimed, mud-spattered, swarthy-visaged, leather-legginged, two-weeks-bearded, sleeveless-armed, pipe-pendant fellows, who could not be coaxed back East nor bribed with anything except a harder job. One covets the cleverness of those rough giants; he envies them their brawn and muscle and he concedes to them the brains their business makes imperative. They are men of stature, these strong-hearted, straight-backed, nimble-witted fellows, these men who have put the "grand" in the Denver and Rio Grande.

Missions.   The second, is the discovery of gold;
the old days of the Argonauts.   The third, is its
wonderful development since the American settlement; the days of planting its orchards of lemons
and oranges, its groves of olive and fig trees, its
vineyards and its fields of grain.   Its earliest days
are recalled on every hand.   Relics of them are
these old Franciscan Missions, twenty-one marvelous structures, thoroughly in keeping with the
country.   The old romantic road connecting them
still serves the modern world.   The second period
was one of quite as thrilling romances; while the
third is being lived and acted out to-day.

Few outsiders realize the immense size of this
State as a whole; such an empire it is in itself.
One illustration of that size is the diversity of
things within it, the extremes that it possesses.
For example, Mount Whitney is the highest point
in the United States, with its crest 14,502 feet
above the sea; while the lowest spot on the American Continent also is here, the Salton Sea, 287 feet
below sea level.   There are such differences in height
as that between the labyrinthian railway over
Mount Tamalpais and the floor of the Yosemite
Valley.   There are mounds of lava from extinct

volcanoes and there are deep valleys where verdure is fresh the whole year round. There are Keersage Pinnacles, veritable roof of the United States, and there are Coronado Beach and Catalina Islands, its front doorstep and its patio. There are the biggest trees in the world and the smallest, the most dainty of flowers. There are giant cactuses and there are the blossoms proverbially worn by brides.

All these contrasts and extremes you surmise when you cross the mountains at the border, rising from the low level Mojave Desert on one side and dropping down hard by San Bernardino on the other. Here is the place where farmers derive ultimately yellow metal from the air and Apples of Hesperides lie on the ground. This portion of the journey is like nothing else that I remember so much as the trip across northern Italy eastward to Venice—after coming down the Alps upon the plain north of Verona. Nowhere else save there is such green and such gold at once; nor are there anywhere else such long, straight, level roads.

On this perfect grade, apparently intoxicated with view and environs, the locomotive quickens its speed and with accelerating rate new features come on in the landscape. I recall a heightening enthusiasm over palms, green plots of grass, level roads, flowers, bungalows, hotels, tropical varieties of every plant and shrub, concrete work, crowds, sunshine, sprinkling of water, automobiles, more autos, trolley lines, climate, more trolleys, and more climate. These I jotted down as they passed the car window—and we arrived in Los Angeles.

On the next day we betook ourselves adown the coast toward San Diego, through that ancient country to this modern exposition. The way leads through the orange belt, along the famous Foothills Boulevard whence motorists may enjoy the entire journey from Riverside to San Diego along the foot of the Sierra Madre, to the California Exposition city. But, even without a motor, the journey is a delight by train. Looking in all directions the impressive feature is the regularity, rectangularity of everything. All roads lie, as all fences stand, and as for that matter, all things grow in lines as straight as beams of sunlight: small fruits, trees, telegraph poles, fences, roads, irrigation trenches, railroad tracks. Even the oil derricks seem to follow on top of a stream of wealth that, although subterranean, flows in as straight a

Old Mission of San Juan Capistrano

line.　There are miles on miles of flat, interminable
orange groves, so also of lemon and citrus, then
wheat fields denuded, but their straw baled eco-
nomically and not burned as in the wasteful Northwest, clumps of more windmills, more oil derricks,
and then whitewashed, carefully constructed
cattle pens enticing beeves to market by the
myriad.

On we go, close down the shore of the Pacific,
where the long, white water-windrows roll in hard
against the cliffs; while both the blue sky and the
bluer sea look like innumerable pictures one has
seen of both.　We hit the trail of the old padres,
the ancient El Camino Real, the old-time King's
Highway, along which the Spaniards traveled.　It
lies along the whole slope of the coast from San
José.　Of the Missions themselves, the most
picturesque is old San Juan Capistrano.　In the
year the Fathers of our Country signed the Declara-
tion of Independence, the Fathers of the Church
established this Station of the Cross, sixty-five
miles south of what is now Los Angeles.　It was
located upon a circle of hills overlooking a beautiful
valley leading to the ocean.　Indians did the work,
but the long lines of arches, massive in stone

and mortar, are still admired by the architect and engineer.

The Exposition is, of course, San Diego's overwhelming attraction; but there are many other things of interest to do and see. There are excursions to the Coronado Islands, trips to Romana's Home in the old Spanish quarter, little journeys to Otay and Sweetwater Dams, to El Cajon and the Hidden Valley. Madam Tingley's Theosophical Institute adds a touch of enticement, as it lends a note of color, to Point Loma. Coronado Beach forms the bulwark between the blue sea and the wide bay, while a government boulevard leads out to the gigantic headland that shoulders its way for a full dozen miles out to sea. Here still stands the old Spanish Lighthouse, the highest in the United States, and here also are both the Government Wireless Station and Fort Rosecrans, where a battalion of coast artillery man the big ten-inch guns that guard the entrance to the harbor.

It was Juan Rodriquez Cabrillo who discovered San Diego in 1542, although the settlement of the coast country did not begin till 1769. Of that later settlement there is suitable commemoration in a memorial tablet to "Fray Junipero and his fellow-pioneers, whose saintly devotion and daunt-less courage established Christianity and civiliza-tion in Alta California." From the moment that you cross the Puento to the Exposition you see only beauty. Whether you look from the east side of the Alameda, or beyond the Citrus Orchard; whether you look on the Pepper Grove of flowers in beauty or the model intensive farm, epitome in itself of utility; whether you look eastward in El Prado, from the Plaza de Panama, or at the foun-tain by La Laguna Espejada (the Mirror Pool) or La Laguna de las Flores (the Pool of Flowers), from the edge of La Canada de las Palmas (the Palm Jungle) or down in the Kiva (cave) in the Painted Desert of old Santa Fé, or off the edge of the Canyon Español toward Taos Pueblo, or at the group of State buildings on La Via de los Estados, in the quiet patios of all which flowers bloom and fountains play—it is all the same. And you breathe a sigh of gratitude to think that, when last single summer's exposition has long closed its gates, when the temporary buildings of the Panama Pacific Exposition up in San Francisco have been razed, when 1915 has passed into oblivion, this

magnificent testimonial of love for the Sunny
Southland and devotion to the erstwhile padres,
this Balboa Park, still remains. And it shall
remain, to be enjoyed for generations, by visitors
to this City of the Harbor of the Sun.

CHAPTER XVII

Camp Life in Yosemite Valley

 HAVE been to all the chief resorts, I think, in the United States where Nature's wonders are made centers for sightseeing. I have essayed descriptions of them through three years professionally. I am glad I put off this trip to Yosemite until the last, for it is climax to the whole; it is as different from each of the others as it is superior to all of them in its peculiar forms of fascination.

Elsewhere one catches piecemeal an impression of the scale upon which Nature does things, reveals her marvels, and reserves surprises. One who travels east or west transcontinentally learns the wide reaches of the prairies, the height to which mountains may be piled, the density of forests, width of rivers, charm of valleys, and sonorous sound of waterfalls, the size of trees, and above all, the age thus indicated, the antiquity, stern dignity, and repose of illimitable time and imperturbable silence. Here, however, one finds all these things at once.

While the Yosemite may well be the last place to visit in a series—if one follows a progressive order and would work up to a climax—it was one of the first regions of our great natural wonder lands to be made into a national park. It is more than forty years now since it began to attract tourists. But its interest has grown rather than diminished. That is why this is the "big thing" to do out here. The Yosemite and the Big Trees together—these are Mecca, it would seem, for every pilgrim who on his route east or west goes perforce north or south through one or other of two junctions whence the journey may be made with ease.

A plateau is at the bottom of the Valley, as flat and extensive as you would climb hills to attain elsewhere. The peaks and summits are great sawed-off buttresses which taper downward, so that sides of mountains seem not only to stand straight but to lean over backward toward you. Away off above are the vast meadows of the sky, dotted with sheaves of cloud on the blue background as white themselves as the flower-covered carpet where you lie is blue.

About you everywhere there are choice spots for camps with dense forest for shade underlooking peaceful valleys high up in the air. And there are camps also, as many as places. Indeed, there is no other way of living for those who would sojourn in this out-of-doors. There are admirable permanent camps, as big as army encampments. And they have all the needful accessories: automobiles and stages, four-horse coaches, saddle horses, telephones, electric lights, and all other conveniences, insuring a delightful stay of a day or a week or a month in the mountains. Hereabouts are half a dozen tented cities. Here is a metropolis of canvas in the center of the wilderness. Here are a post-office, express, telephone, and telegraph offices, office of the superintendent of the park, a general store, and all kinds of curio emporiums. With amazing resourcefulness, every detail has been arranged for comfort, for convenience, and for cleanliness.

The joys here of camp life are commingled with every device known to the city habitant. There are swimming pools, dancing pavilions, baseball grounds, tennis courts, bowling alleys, soda fountains, laundries, yes, and "movies." Think of a Palace Hotel turned into a 1000-square mile public park, the lobby made of rustic logs of firs, the carpets deep pine needles, the orchestra a mountain stream, the heating system a camp-fire of cedar logs, and the illumination a million living firebrands dropping from a cliff 3000 feet above your head and you may gain an idea of this forest hostelry.

In this camp the "help" are largely from the colleges. A very fine lot of young people, Western college boys and co-eds, waited on our tables and toted our baggage, sweatered, blazered, badged, and decorated in their négligé attire with every form of athletic and Hellenic monogram and cryptogram. To say that the guests could not be told from the help was, upon the whole, a compliment to the guests.

Here was a sample in truth of a shirt-sleeve democracy. In all of these camps last night, put together, 5000 people slept, not to say without a lock on a door—for there is hardly a door in the Valley—but with scarcely so much as a tent flap closed. There was a motley variety of guests, rich, poor, old, young, wise and otherwise, who sat around great camp-fires and at nine o'clock withdrew to soundest slumber.

Which, most of all, reminds me: one must see the Valley in the moonlight. I had lain awake and listened to the music while, there in the wilderness, hundreds of people danced. I waked again to hear the sound of the wind in the trees, and yet again was wakened by the very silence—it was so intense. If one is to use a night like this for sleep he must sleep soon and soundly; for the early intrusion of the morning mountain light is as surprising as the twilight was long, slow, and lingering. But this night happened to be that of the full moon and, in that weird light, the cliffs had a charm and made an appeal it would have been a desecration to sleep through.

I dressed and went forth stealthily. I wandered at will where the only sound was not a sound at all, but the far echo of the sound of falling waters and the only sights were shadows rather which the darkness but made visible. If you ever have the luck to tread the meadows where the Asphodel shall grow and where Lethe itself will pour its life-giving post-mortem stream, you may have this experience. But, if by any chance you fear you may miss that, then go to Yosemite. And, having decided to go, plan to go in the August full moon—and stay over night.

The next day I went on a visit to the famed Big Trees. They are calculated to impress first by their size but in the end most by their age. Older than our modern customs, older than our oldest usage, underneath semblance of change and back of every shifting circumstance that breaks up into tiny cycles the brief span of any single lifetime as a whole, there are qualities of permanence, dim shadows of eternity, for one who but opens his eyes to see them, in this scene of Nature's setting in a land from which I have but recently returned.

As there flit to and fro in the brief memory of one short passing lifetime the successive turning points that mark the years, my thought goes off to this sense of abiding permanence—engendered by groves of big trees. These Sequoias Giganteas are found only in the Sierra Nevada Mountain Range. They grow to a height of 350 feet, and occasionally have a base circumference of more than one hundred feet. Their age is determined by counting the annular rings from the center,

The Floor of the Yosemite Valley

each ring indicating a year's growth. When John Muir, the well-known California scientist, carefully examined one of these trees, burned part way through, it was found by these concentric growths to be more than 6000 years of age. They are thus the oldest as well as the largest living things in the world.

Indeed the Trees are more wonderful than the Valley because they live and grow. Their chief wonder is that they have been living so long. They represent a continuous life that began on the farther side of history. Their magnificent proportions and the awful solitudes in which they dwell give them a sublime grandeur. They are the only known form of living vegetation that seem to have the power to heal their own scars indefinitely, to have no natural death, to be as nearly, as living things can be, immortal. They have thus the power to breathe upon one a great peace; for they "make our noisy years seem moments in the being of eternal silence."

There are three main groves of these Big Trees within the limits of the park, the Tuolumne, Merced, and Mariposa. But to see one is of course to have seen all. The best way to arrange this as a part of one composite trip is by the new so-called Triangular Route. This auto road has only recently been opened and the journey over it requires but four hours' extra time of one's itinerary. Here is a wonderful scenic trip, through forest and over mountain, by stream and waterfall, and then a long ascent. For you must ascend far by a corkscrew, switchback, and circuitous course naturally to get up and out of the Valley to the far high forests where these giants dwell. The views from the road itself are entrancing. Vistas and panoramas open before you at every turn. Now you are looking down the cañon, the river a mere silver line in the rich green of the vast forest growth. Again the view looks off toward the main entrance to the park, guarded by sheer granite cliffs and towering mountain slopes. Across the cañon spreads the vast timber belt, with all the Valley's five falls in sight in the distance. On you go, through virgin forests, the air balmy with the odor of pines and firs, until at the end of a couple of hours you arrive at Tuolumne Grove, in reaching which you have climbed over 7000 feet above sea level.

The most striking tree of the Tuolumne Grove is

the "Dead Giant," through a tunnel in which the auto passes. This was the first big tree in the world to be tunnelled and the method gives a proper idea of its diameter, which is more than thirty feet, with an opening ten feet square. It has been estimated by scientists that the living height of the "Dead Giant," before it became a stump as now, was five hundred feet and, with the bark, at least forty feet in diameter. This was undoubtedly the largest tree in the world at that time. It was destroyed, by lightning evidently, some three hundred years ago and yet I drove through the stump of it but yesterday. The Grizzly Giant, 104 feet in circumference, is estimated to be 8000 years old. The Fallen Monarch is the one upon whose hulk, now prone, but towering before Cheops built his pyramid, are driven a stage full of sight-seers, drawn by six horses; and all have ample room to go in safety and in comfort.

The first discovery of big trees was made in October, 1849, by Major Burney, then Sheriff of Mariposa County. He came across a few of them, forming part of a group in what is now known as the Fresno Grove. Thereafter, from time to time, persons exploring the mountains found grove after grove, until it was known that groups of them were scattered along the western front of the Sierras for a distance of about two hundred miles. These forest giants, by the mere doctrine of chance, must have been exposed to forest fires, not once, but many times. And while they are not absolutely fireproof, the fact that they have stood there through so many ages shows that they must be decidedly fire-resistant. Nearly every tree is scarred at the base by fire; but still it lives. The Sequoia has no diseases, never decays, cannot be blown down, and does not burn up. That is the reason it outlives everything else in existence.

The whole Yosemite National Park, of which the Valley and these Trees are only two incidents, is as vast as it is comprehensive. The mere journey to it, even from the junction on a main trans-continental line, is a short side journey that may be made easily. It is a wonderful experience, this journey to the high Sierras, a charming hegira, through vast virgin forests; for in the way there are seen spreading panoramas and vistas of mountain peaks, tumbling waterfalls, granite heights, cascades, and river scenes unparalleled in all the world.

The hills are the chief things in sight, and there are some thousand square miles of them; but the Valley proper, even with all these hills, is but part of a National Park. This latter embraces the whole crest of the Sierras, a territory of 1124 square miles.

I will not attempt comparison with other places save at the length of one illustration. At the Grand Canyon, in Arizona, you are at the edge of the world looking down and in; here you are at the bottom, looking out and always up. The first is a place to sojourn; this second is a place wherein you need not loiter to gain inspiration you will long remember. One can make the whole trip in and out comfortably in two days. The place is too big to be spoiled. It has power to overwhelm the most experienced globe-trotters, with its miles of perpendicularity.

It is supreme in charm and in beauty; but it is something else as well. It is majestic and awe-inspiring. The awful grandeur of those rivers, rushing off precipices thousands of feet high and the sublimity of those stupendous cliffs, springing vertically from the level valley floor, are relieved and softened by charms of rich verdure and of golden sunlight.   Its beauty is no less but no more notable than its majesty.   It has no rival on earth for its many natural attractions and points of interest for merely *blasé* travelers; but it has a value in the field also of worship and devotion. Here the weary rest; but here also the poet is inspired, the artist is entranced, and the priest has a new reason for becoming pious.   It is no wonder that it has been called the Cathedral of the Almighty.   That half dome, towering in the clouds, is the background to a giant altar; that fragrance of the flowers is incense and the wind is the diapason of a true choir invisible.

CHAPTER XVIII

Study of Some Types of Tourists

AM on a five days' journey straightway from east to west across the continent. I have, on other journeys, found much interest in sights and scenes, in things and places; this time, I confess, I am more interested in observing people. On a journey such as this, there is much to be studied in the book of human nature.

It was David Harum who observed: "There is as much human nature in some people as there is in others—if not a little more." In such summer travel, sometimes far from home, what there is latent in people comes to the surface. In this Western land there are conditions, and within the circumstances of such travel there are reasons why one with a penchant for the chiefest study of mankind—which Pope has said is man—can sit still and see humanity rotate about him. It is

173

for this reason I am moved to make this Study of Some Types of Tourists.

In our party there are groups of all of a dozen well-known types. There are those who regard the journey in every possible way; from the man who has been over the same route so many times that he spends his time merely in trying to pass it in comfort, from the crowds who are either too incompetent to appreciate the scenery or so uninterested as to disregard it and who spend the days, instead of viewing it, in playing bridge— from those down to the children who, with open mouths and eager eyes of wonder, take in everything, and thus gain "knowledge never learned in school."

There are those who represent all grades of culture and refinement also; from the elderly man, well-known, well-groomed, well-preserved, whose garb bespeaks wealth, whose manner bespeaks gentility, who is truly "to the manner born," and who has learned that it pays to "be gentle and keep your voice low"—to those of the very opposite extreme, whose vulgar ostentation and tasteless display make them, whether at home or abroad, the laughingstock of the social world. There are those, too, who show plainly how much or how little they have traveled; from the worldly-wise commercial traveler, whose route takes him monthly over two thousand miles in circuit and who has lived on the cars until he could almost run a railroad himself, down to the woman who watches the telegraph wires to see if she can see a message going by.

There are young folk, traveling alone, representatives of Young America; from the broad-shouldered, peg-top-trousered youth, who with hands in pockets, pipe pendant, countenance couchant, and keen eyes rampant, does not need the triangular shaped flag pin on his coat lapel to tell what college he hails from, to the young lady with the regulation gesture of her carefully manicured fingers tucking back a refractory curl, studiously naïve and self-consciously unconscious that every-one in the car is conscious of her presence, who with baggage in abundance and the smile that won't come off, is returning home from one of many Eastern boarding schools.

There are those, too, who are restless in as many ways; from the woman who between every two stations half a hundred miles apart writes letters home, to the man who spends his time in walking up and down the aisle composing telegrams to send off at as many stations to his office. And there are those who are laboriously studious in many ways, eager to make the most of the journey; from the lady clamoring for statistics, who sits all day with notebook in one hand and guide-book in the other, asking everyone who comes in range, just where we are now, just what is the altitude here, the height of that mountain there, the width of that river or the length of that bridge, down to the professional hack-writer off on a journey to write up the country for his city editor, the true type of laborious journalist.

> Writing for the papers,
>   Which, as everyone knows,
> Is worse than keeping chickens,
>   Or scaring off the crows.

I remember once to have heard two small boys discussing the professions they would choose. The one decided—"I will be an astronomer." "But," cried the other, "what will you do all day long?" I had often found myself wondering what people traveling on so long a journey would do all day long. How would one ever pass the time? The simple truth is one does nothing, and is well content to do it. We sit and read by hours the book of travel, whose pages are miles of changing landscape and look into galleries of genre pictures framed in square car windows.

The time does not seem long; it passes so quickly that all times we are well content to turn our watches back an hour a day. There are, of course, the regulation things to do, the doing of which marks the progress of the day. One rises late or early as he pleases. Shortly a newsboy appears from some mysterious place with papers taken at dead night from the nearest city, whether Buffalo, Chicago, Denver, or Salt Lake; the news from all the world is brought as promptly to one's breakfast table as would be the case at home.

It is after dinner, in the smoking car, that the men are at their best—and happiest. The conditions here are precisely those that would prevail at home, at any dinner party. And the test of manhood here as there is still the same; namely, the man is most a man who can continue to be popular among men after the ladies have gone. It is here that conversation worthy of the name begins.

12

Here, too, the order of procedure is the same as at home; the man with least to say begins to talk soonest; the wise ones sit in silence and allow him to exhaust himself. Of the former, there are all the usual types: there is the boastful man who tells of his wealth and possessions at home; there is the contentious man who never has learned finesse and who in argument addresses himself with a sledge hammer to a point which a tack hammer would crush; there are the complaining ones, from the fussy old man describing his rheumatic pains to the blatant Englishman lamenting that, "the bath arrangements on these trains are so poor, don't you know?" There is the man who will not talk at all, no matter how you press him; and there is the one who will do nothing but talk, no odds how you repress him.

But, after all this has passed,—and it passes with the smoke that it resembles—a chance expression here and there drops hint of who the other men are and of what their business is. There is the promoter, easily recognized from his use of the word "proposition"; there is the foreign representative, who remarks casually, "A month hence when I am in Australia"; while other remarks indicate

Automobile Road on the Desert

past histories of interest and travels over lands, the tales of which would fascinate the most *blasé*. In one group one night on this train, for instance, one man was a civil service officer; one man a detective in the Government employ—a special agent of the Post Office Department, on his way to Honolulu to investigate the sending of explosives through the mail; another was a typical Owen Wister Virginian, dressed in a corduroy suit, with a Colt revolver and a quiet manner, on his way into the far West to pass judgment on some big timber and there was a surveyor who had helped to build that section of this very railroad that lies over the Rocky Mountains.

And once more, even, if possible, more interesting still, are the people we see from the car windows, whether in the loneliness of the prairie's wide expanse or in those centers of pseudo-civilization, the towns. I have learned to understand the surprise of Robert Louis Stevenson, who wondered at those who could find time heavy on their hands in waiting at a railway station, "As though there were no people to look at." People themselves are always worth looking at, and so many of them as one can see on so long a journey are especially so. I have learned to understand, too, what he meant who said: "I am never quite sure of life unless I can see literature in it."

If one will go on the assumption that there is a skeleton in every family closet and at least one romance still unwritten in every life, he will find in the sight of so many lives, themes and material for novels by the score. Curious and interesting is the sight of that admixture of people waiting at so many stations all along the way. There are the employees themselves, nonchalant baggage men, ticket agents with their air of *savoir faire*, the people who have come to see their friends or neighbors off, and those who have come merely to see the train in and out, the whole mixture being diluted here and there, in the far West, by an Indian, a Chinese, a lumberjack, and a cowboy.

For, to see the West without seeing a cowboy would surely be "'Hamlet' with Hamlet left out." He is both in fact and fancy the most picturesque figure of the present, as he was of the former, life of the far West. In novels he does three things: he works, he plays, and he makes love. In real life, as well, he does all three, and he does each with a will, but he never allows any two of them to conflict. The mundane duties of a practical cow-puncher are unromantic in the extreme and strenuous to the last degree. It is the resourcefulness and faithfulness with which, in the absence of elaborate equipment, and unconstrained by the eye of an overseeing employer, he discharges the duties that fall to his lot that compel one's admiration.

CHAPTER XIX

The Westward Course of Empire

HERE is something so fairly awesome in the vast expanse of territory that one sees unfolded as one travels to and fro across the continent, and so solemnly impressive in the greatness of his native country when one sees it thus unrolling itself like a huge map of three million square miles in area that observation turns to a peculiar kind of admiration, which makes eulogy into a higher form of praise; it turns patriotism, and rightly, into a veritable form of religion itself.

It is necessary to review a little of our geography and to rehearse some facts of history. It is worth while to trace first, in a word or two, the history by epochs of the geographical enlargement of this country; next to rehearse, also in a paragraph, the names of those few men who were responsible for this—men who took a prophetic view of their country's possibilities—and, as a third attempt, to show that the fortunes of this country, are, in this generation especially, being committed in trust to those who happen in the present to know most about the past.

Everyone knows that the territory of the Thirteen Colonies, embraced under the Federal Constitution at the date of that Constitution's adoption in 1783, was a narrow, crooked little strip of land, the width of which was the distance only from the Eastern seaboard to the Appalachian chain. They know that the main additions to this have been about half a dozen. These may be recalled to memory, as thus:

All know that the first of these additions was by the Ordinance of 1787, that ordinance which amounted virtually to a secondary Constitution, by which the several Colonies ceded to the Federal Government the Northwest Territory—that triangular strip lying between the Ohio, the Great Lakes, and the Mississippi River, comprising to-day the States of Ohio, Indiana, Illinois, Michigan, and Wisconsin.

They know that, in 1803, the purchase was made for $15,000,000 of that 900,000 square miles of land which, by the Treaty of Paris, in 1763, France had given to Spain, but which by the secret Treaty of Ildefonso, in 1801, Spain had given back to France, and which, because it offered a menace to his plans at home, Napoleon was willing to deed to us "forever and in full sovereignty," that vast territory stretching from the Mississippi River to the crest of the Rocky Mountains, and from the Gulf of Mexico to the border line of Canada—a territory as large as England, Ireland, Scotland, France, Spain, Germany, the Netherlands, Italy, and Switzerland all combined.

They know that, in 1819, the trouble which had arisen a few years earlier from certain vigorous proceedings on the part of American citizens in the Southern Peninsula, where the Spaniards either could not or would not keep the Seminoles in order, was adjusted by the purchase of Florida from Spain for $5,000,000, that tract extending off southeast which some one of his day prophetically called "The Index Forefinger of the Continent Beckoning Cuba."

They know that, in 1845, Texas was annexed, it having achieved its independence in the defeat of Santa Anna, in 1836, and having continued thereafter in separate civic entity as "The Lone

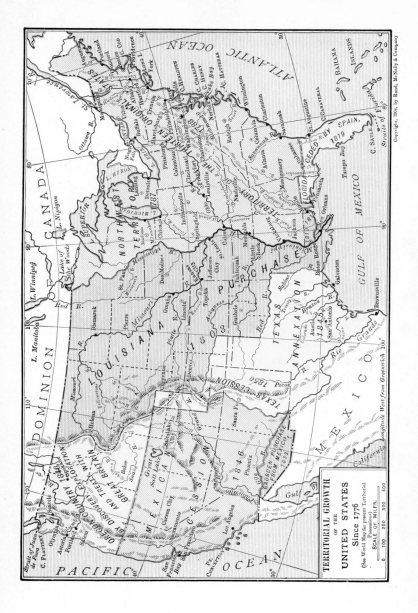

TERRITORIAL GROWTH
OF THE
UNITED STATES
Since 1776
(See World Map for present Territorial
Possessions.)
SCALE OF MILES.
0   100   200   300   400

Copyright, 1904, by Rand, McNally & Company

Star State." They know that, in 1846, Oregon, although held by us conjointly with Great Britain since 1818, had its boundary line determined by treaty with England, that land projected on a scale commensurate in size with its own "winds, rivers, mountains, and forests." And they know that, in 1848, California, upon the concluding of peace with Mexico, was had by us for an indemnity of $15,000,000.

But all this did not do itself. Therefore, it is necessary to rehearse, as in a second group, the names of the men who did it. They were men truly possessed of second sight and that of extraordinary quality. Their greatness appears especially to-day in proportion as they stood out in opposition to their own contemporaries. For they not only saw far ahead of their time, but they had to contend for their vision. For example, in 1780, in a discussion of the question of the public lands, Lord Hillsborough scouted the idea that there would ever be salable land "at the back of Virginia."

It was Thomas Paine, strangely enough, among the prophets here who replied: "Sir, I tell you that the mapmakers may as well sharpen their

tools; for there is going to be work for them to do."
In contrast to those at home who deprecated the
proceeding, there stands out the splendid diplo-
macy of Benjamin Franklin, John Jay, and John
Adams, our negotiators abroad, in securing for
us that imperial domain, the Northwest Territory,
when the treaty with Great Britain was drawn in
1783. Again when Talleyrand urged upon Spain
the relinquishment of Louisiana and Florida, proposing to make of them "a wall forever im-
penetrable to the combined efforts of England
and America," it was Thomas Jefferson who saw
in their possession a chance for the ascendancy of
the Anglo-Saxon race on the Western Hemisphere.

When he began by seeking merely a shipping
port, there were those who objected to his paying
even $2,000,000 for it.   But he saw " . . . in that
'Mobile country' a commercial entrepôt for all
the commodities of the exterior. . . ."   When he
asked for this single port and had an empire thrust
upon him, such men as White and Pickering and
Tracy objected, with one voice, in public debate
in the Senate, to "the payment of $15,000,000 for
a wilderness."   But Jefferson saw that the Mississippi River ought to be controlled throughout

its entire length by one nation, and that the land along its course was worth at least two and a half cents an acre. He saw, too, that to delay would be to put the whole acquisition to hazard; so he bought it, on his own responsibility, even though to do so he had to desert his own strict constructionist theory, and venture upon an exercise of power as bold as Hamilton's assumption of state debts.

And there were others of a wholly different class. The fact is that, in the eye of history, statesmen and diplomatists often usurp more than their proper share of compliment. In reality they only bring to a conclusion movements started by adventurous spirits before them. One may well pause to pay tribute to all those—adventurers, discoverers, explorers, settlers—who cut the trails across the continent and set up stakes which others reached forth to, and by which they drew themselves on.

I have in mind the work of Daniel Boone, who in going to Kentucky, in 1769, was the first man who ever led a body of settlers to establish a community completely cut off from the seaboard colonies. I am thinking of General Rufus Putnam, who crossed the Ohio in 1788, and who, in believing that others would follow, was as bold in his faith as Columbus the day he put forth from Palos. I have in mind George Rogers Clark's Conquest of the Illinois, in 1778—the young explorer sent out by Patrick Henry, then Governor of Virginia. I am thinking of Zebulon Montgomery Pike, who, in 1805, reached the source of the Mississippi, settled there, and became the precursor of the famous Rocky Mountain Men.

And of course I am thinking of the expedition of Lewis and Clark sent out by Jefferson in 1804 to explore Oregon, which exploration formed a strong link in our claim to that land later; while time would fail me to tell of Hamilton and Robertson, of Isaac Shelby and Simeon Kenton, of John Sevier and Anthony Wayne and of their valor at Marietta and Vincennes, at Muskingum and the Great Kanawha, at King's Mountain and the Fallen Timbers. Nor would time alone, but words, fail me to tell of those who followed these, the great deeds done in the conquest of the wilderness by that race of restless and intrepid pioneers who, with the gunsmith and the saddler for their only outfitters, with the sun for their only companion by day, and the sky for their tent by night, with instinct for a guide and high hope for a canopy moved westward, ever westward, fighting climate and disease, the wild beasts of the forest and its wilder human denizens; who drove that enemy— the frontier—from one ocean clear to the other, until to-day they have set looms and anvils in the haunts and lairs of beasts, until cities are reared in the bosom of solitude itself, and quarter-sections are now staked for sale above old Indian graves.

CHAPTER XX

Men who Matched their Mountains

AVING crossed the continent from the Atlantic to the Pacific this summer, as several times before, and now having crossed the border and traversed a thousand miles or more of Canada on this vacation journey, I find it not only difficult but absolutely impossible, now sitting down to write, to think of things conventional or to refrain from rapture over the bigness of the land that I have ridden over.

A mere study of his country's vastness makes one humble to the point of being meditative. If one thinks devoutly, one will find himself in a mood so religious that to speak of his country in eulogy is not to boast so much as it is to exult with a kind of holy exultation; he will thank his God for this His goodness, manifest in greatness, and that most of all in generosity, in giving in this vast new Western world such a rich heritage that he should study to prove worthy of it.

More than that even, one is impressed with a feeling of gratitude for the great men who have made this composite country what it has come to be. It is hard to be moderate here. And perhaps one is not called upon to be. Great things have been done which did not do themselves. The stereotyped falsities of history are very many in America. They creep upon us unawares. Maybe, rather, we accept them with our eyes wide open; it is so easy and so pleasant to commingle fact with fiction, to mistake the legendary for the literal. But here is a realm where, instead of fiction being presented for fact, the facts are such as to assume the air of fiction.

And there is no need for jealousy. There is glory enough to go around. One feels the same in Canada that he does in the United States. Nor yet again are there permissible limits in one's praise set by the bounds of denominations. Rome had part in this as well as Geneva. The Spanish Conquistadores and the French Padres, as well as the Scotch-Irish colporteur and Church of England missionary. There are pages by the score of Park-

man that tell true tales wilder than the untrue tales
of Cooper.   There were deeds done in the Northwest that deified men in the doing.   There were
early Voyageurs who dared death with an iron
courage, men who played games with kings and
with continents for stakes.   There were *coureurs
de bois* who tamed the wilderness, fighting alike
the forests and their wilder human denizens.
There were Jesuits, aye, there were Nuns—who
lived with the self-abnegation of saints and died
with the devotion of martyrs.

In both lands, north and south of parallel
"forty-nine fifty," where the portions are but
roughly defined and the settlements far separated,
where the parts are only thinly populated and the
whole expanse comparatively lately peopled, if at
all, quite naturally there are types of human kind
—as well as types of mountain, river, forest, beast,
and bird—both notable and curious.   There are
names well known and oft-quoted of persons,
fabled as well as famous, both of those long dead
and of those now living, of olden-time adventurers
and present-time habitués, early explorers, found-
ers, settlers, as likewise of present-day patrons of
prominence.   Every region has unwritten stories

of odd pioneers and *outré* characters, told only by night around the camp-fire, writ largely only upon leaves of the library of local tradition.

Each district, too, has its idol, or its ideal, its object of hero worship, its patron saint for devotion, its model for emulation, be he millionaire, mechanic, mining man, or ranchman, in what way soever he has become famous or favored or a favorite. Of these, chiefest are the projectors, promoters, financiers, and builders of the great railroads. For the true empire builders out here were the men who made an empire habitable. These were they who linked it up by iron rails and tied it with telegraph lines to other older seats of human habitation.

And there were other factors still, other commercial factors, in producing this great change. On that day, in 1806, when Pike sighted that giant peak which has served as a magnet to draw adventurous spirits ever since; on that day, in 1848, when James Marshall picked up that pebble in the raceway of Sutter's mill, on the American fork of the Sacramento, a discovery which set up such a peaceful migration as the world had never seen; on that day when Fairweather and Edgar made their strike in Alder Gulch, the thing that put Montana on the map; on that day, in 1869, when the rails of the Union and Central Pacific railroads met at Promontory Point, completing the first of those mighty highways that have quickened every movement of commercial enterprise and social intercourse; then and there, on those days and in those places was history made.   The whole is a long story, but it is full of charm, for it is the story of those who went forth in faith; of those who through faith subdued kingdoms, wrought righteousness, quenched the violence of fire, escaped the edge of the sword, out of weakness were made strong, waxed valiant in fight, put to flight the armies of the aliens; which things declare plainly that they sought a country.   They sought it and they found it.

There are three things essential for any one who would form a worthy estimate now of his country to base gratitude upon.   First, it is necessary to take a large enough view of our country's possibilities; to be credulous of its future.   While this continent was unknown, imagination peopled it with strange creatures and filled it with a wealth immeasurable.   It was the Orient; in it were Elixir and the Philosopher's Stone; El Dorado, Coronado, Bonanza, Cibola, and the Seven Cities. Now that it has been explored the facts outrun all former fancies. Its size, its wealth, its growth are fairly fabulous. Its area, doubled and quadrupled many times; its population, multiplied one hundred-fold in just about one hundred years; its national wealth of full a hundred billion dollars—why, these things put the legends of mythology to shame.

Secondly, it is necessary to take a balanced view; to avoid provincialism. Mr. Emerson once remarked: "I call him a great man who has only to open his eyes to see things in a clear light, in right relation, and in due perspective." This is certainly a mark of greatness, but it is a mark about as rare in possession as it is distinctive in quality. Not to see things thus is to be provincial. And it is to be feared that, of such provincialism, our Eastern States, especially their cities, are most full. At the celebration of the fiftieth anniversary of the Pacific University in Oregon a few years ago, the orator of the day startled the press of the country by declaring that: "After all, it is the residents of the far East who are provincial, and those of the far West who are really cosmopolitan." In large measure he was right. Provincialism is not a thing, but a way of looking at things.

In the third place, it is necessary to take what I can call by no better name than a fair view. Perhaps I can best make plain what I mean by quoting Cromwell's famous exhortation to his troops: "I beseech you, brethren, by the tender mercies of the Lord, that ye conceive it possible that sometimes even ye might be mistaken." I am moved to plead this point because of the way to-day so many men seem prone to approve, on the other hand, Decatur's famous sentiment: "My country, right or wrong."

It is possible that, at times, our Country may be wrong. There have been times when it has been wrong. And there may be such again. It is the part of greatness at such times to see this and to admit it. The great men of every land have been those who were great enough in any case to see this and confess it. Did not such patriots as Burke and Chatham protest against the war of England with her American colonies? Did not Lord Salisbury say: "In going into the Crimean War for the support of Turkish despotism, England put her money on the wrong horse?" Did not such men as Mr. Morley, Mr. Bryce, and Sir William Vernon Harcourt protest against the recent South African War, deprecating its origin and criticizing its course? And did not all the best men in the United States, including Mr. Lincoln, protest throughout against our early war with Mexico? We can do this in our own age, only by studying our country's history. And, in that study, we must go to original sources—to documents and state papers. Do this. Do it with a desire, not to justify your country's actions, but to weigh them. Thus, and thus only, will one avoid Dr. Johnson's opprobrium—"Patriotism? The last refuge of a scoundrel."

THE END